MW01167283

Who Cares?
"WHEN THE SAINTS COME MARCHING IN"

FINDING SOBRIETY "THE TRUTH" AND HAPPINESS

by
Thomas John Ford

authorHOUSE

AuthorHouse™
1663 Liberty Drive, Suite 200
Bloomington, IN 47403
www.authorhouse.com
Phone: 1-800-839-8640

First published by AuthorHouse 6/25/2009

ISBN: 978-1-4259-0795-2 (sc)

Printed in the United States of America
Bloomington, Indiana

This book is printed on acid-free paper.

FOREWORD

"My journey has taken me to the physical, the meta-physical, the delusional, and back" How much I can identify with those words from a recent movie. The actor who spoke those words was portraying a man with severe schizophrenia. My malady was severe alcoholism. My mental, emotional, and spiritual handicaps were in evidence far before I ever took my first drink. By the end of my drinking career, the professional assessment of my condition was. Thomas J. Ford is either, " retarded" or "demonized"! I am alive today because a " higher power" spared me. With so much suffering in the world to claim a personal "miracle", makes God seem unfair. It makes me seem self-absorbed. All I know is, I was blind. But now I can see! A extremely wicked king in ancient Israel is the Bible character who closely mirrors my life and experiences. His name was Manasseh, Who 2 Chronicles 33:6 says : "He did on a grand scale what was bad in the eyes of Jehovah, to offend him" However after much pain and suffering: "Manasseh came to know that Jehovah is the [true] God. From a broken down divorced, unemployed, pee in the bed drunk. To the person on the cover of this book. I hope my story will inspire others, alcoholics and non drinkers. I have pursued the truth of the Bible, with the same zeal I once had for wickedness. I have found the words of Isaiah 55 : 6, 7 to be true. " Seek ye the Lord while he may be found, call ye upon him while he is near; Let the wicked man forsake his way, and the unrighteous man his thoughts; and let him return unto the Lord, and he will have mercy upon him,....he will abundantly pardon"

"Solomon my son, know the God of your father and serve him with a complete heart and a delightful soul; for all hearts Jehovah is searching, and every inclination of the thoughts he is discerning. IF

YOU SEARCH FOR HIM, HE WILL LET HIMSELF BE FOUND BY YOU." 1 Chronicles 28: 9

I freely quote from two translations of the Bible. One old, one new. The Authorized KING JAMES VERSION of 1611, and a modern language, NEW WORLD TRANSLATION of January 1, 1984. Published by the International Bible Students Association. I have come to love it for it's liberal and correct use of the divine name Jehovah. I will also admit that the old English, with it's thees, thous, he spaketh, smitten, smote, teacheth, and shambles? What is a shambles? 1 Corinthians 10 : 25 says : " Whatsoever is sold in the shambles, that eat" Eat what I wondered? In 1611, it was the common jargon for the hustle and bustle of the "meat market"

I continue my search for the true God even now. So far this is what I have found!!

Thomas John Ford

INDEX OF TOPICS

CHAPTER ONE

WHY DO I NEED TO " SEARCH FOR GOD?"

The three word expression; "search for God", is found more than 20 times in the Bible. Frequently in regard to the kings who ruled in ancient Israel. Some good, but mostly bad. Here are a few examples:

At 1 Chronicles 16: 11 the Levites sang a song: " SEARCH for Jehovah and his strength, seek his face constantly"

King Asa told: " Judah to SEARCH for Jehovah the God of their forefathers" 2 Chronicles 14: 4. Later in verse 9 : "Zerah the Ethiopian went out against them with a military force of a million men and three hundred chariots." But in verse 12, 13 "Jehovah defeated the Ethiopians before Asa and before Judah, ...and those of the Ethiopians continued falling down till there was no one alive of them;" (One million is the largest documented number of humans destroyed on a single occasion by God. We can only estimate the number of those who perished in the flood of Noah's day)

After that deliverance by God. Azariah the prophet said: " Hear me, O Asa and all Judah and Benjamin! Jehovah is with you as long as you prove to be with him; and if you SEARCH for him, he will let himself be found by you" 2 Chronicles 15: 2 Then in verse 12 the entire nation: "entered into a covenant to SEARCH for Jehovah the God of their forefathers". Verse 13 says: " anyone that would not SEARCH for Jehovah the God of Israel should be put to death, whether small or great, whether man or woman"

1

2 Chronicles 20 : 3 says king: "Jehoshaphat became afraid and set his face to SEARCH for Jehovah"

Yes it was a matter of life or death, to search for the true God. This important task has been made more difficult by most modern translations of the Bible.

CHAPTER TWO

WHERE IS THE DIVINE "NAME?"

What has happened to it in the scriptures? It used to be there. It must have been there, because there are far to many references to it. They speak of a single "name", and never of names. As if to imply, God has many names and thus omitting one is not important. When I was growing up, there was prayer everyday at the beginning of the school day. We prayed: "Our father which art in heaven, Hallowed be thy name." Matthew 6 : 9 What name I would ask? So would my classmates. We even had a little joke, that God's name was Howard! "Howard be thy name!" Sometimes, we would say the Lord's prayer found at Psalms 23. Verse 3 says: " he leadeth me in the path of righteousness for his NAME'S sake" Who is he? What is his name? The name was there, it must have been removed! Here is how I know. I read all 150 Psalms. Can you count how many times the writers make direct reference to the name? Psalms 5: 1-" let them also that love thy NAME be joyful in thee" Psalms 7: 17-" and will sing praise to the NAME of the Lord most high" Psalms 8: 1-" how excellent is thy NAME in all the earth" Psalms 9: 2-" I will sing praise to thy NAME" Psalms 9 : 10-" they that know thy NAME will put their trust in thee" Psalms 18: 49-" and sing praises unto thy NAME" Psalms 20 : 1, 5-" "The NAME of the God of Jacob defend thee" " rejoice in thy salvation, and in the NAME of our God" Psalms 20 : 22 " I will declare thy NAME unto my brethren" Psalms 25: 11 "For thy NAME'S sake, O Lord" Psalms 31: 3 "therefore for thy NAME'S sake lead me and guide me" Last but not least, Psalms 34: 3 " and let us exalt his NAME together"

Now notice how the 83rd Psalm, first gives a clue, then finally after so many hints, the divine "NAME".(Singular) Psalms 83 : 16, 18 " Fill their faces with shame; that they may seek thy NAME." What Name? " That men may know that thou, whose name is JEHOVAH art the most high over all the earth " Finally the "name" is revealed. I have a question though. Did all the other writers of the book of Psalms, under the influence of Holy Spirit, forget or refuse to use the divine name? Please take the time to look up the rest of these Psalms. (86: 9, 12)--(91: 14--92: 1--99: 3, 6)--(100: 4--102: 15--103: 2) By now you get the point. How do you feel? I was out-raged! That is plagerism! Those people who translated the King James Bible in 1611 are in heaven? It really makes you wonder. Was it an honest mistake or oversight?

Growing up in the 1960's, I often used the American Standard Version Bible. That translation, 50 years ago had the divine name Jehovah in the text over 6, 000 times. However the New American Standard Version, has the divine name in the main text, not once. Zero!! Is that an improvement? What you have left is a translation that includes the names of false demonic Gods, such as: Baal, Chemosh, Marduk, Tammuz, Dagon, Baalzebub, and of course Satan the Devil himself. But no name for the true God?

The name Jehovah has been completely removed from the New King James version. But that is not all! Even more sinister, is how Jesus final prayer with his apostles has been changed at John 17:6, 26. The old King James read:" I have manifested thy NAME" and, "I have declared unto them thy NAME" What name a person would rightly ask? Some modern translations render John 17: 6, 26 : " I have made YOU manifest!" No mention of a NAME, and thus no perplexing questions. How is that an improved translation? What is their real motive? If You Hide the name of God, how is Malachi 3: 16 to be fulfilled? " A book of Remembrance was written before him for them that feared the Lord, and thought upon his NAME". No name for God, then no book of remembrance with your name in it! In ancient manuscripts the name Jehovah is as common as words like "man" or "woman", or even "the". A Hebrew scholar was asked, What did king David say at Psalms 23 :1 Was it, "the Lord is my shepherd", or

" Jehovah is my shepherd "? He admitted it probably was the latter rendering. " Most people are familiar with the " Lord's Prayer", that is why it is rendered that way." How would he feel if his name had been removed? Jehovah, name of the true God.

CHAPTER THREE

I NEARLY DIED LAUGHING--AT UNCLE LEROY'S FUNERAL

I attended a funeral recently. What can I say? You need a great imagination, and a sense of humor to preach a funeral. This rotten no good uncle of mine died. (If I said he was a nice guy, it would be a lie! Now I have to go to heaven to get my $300 bucks) Uncle Leroy had no life insurance. His motto was: "When I die, I want it to be a sad day! For everybody! Put Leroy's picture in a dictionary, under the word; Riff-raff; no definition needed. My uncle Leroy was to black people, what Billy Carter was to white folks. Pride of the family! (Reah right) The preacher got up in the pulpit, and just made up stuff to say good, about Leroy. (The preacher used a french pronunciation, Le'Roy) They ran out of neck braces, because so many people developed whip-lash! The church looked like center court at Wimbledon. Heads swinging back and forth.! "Who the heck, is he talking about? Somebody switched the casket!" A philantropist? Le'Roy? "He ever give you anything?" Nothing but a headache! But just once. Wouldn't it be fun, to go to a funeral, and hear the preacher get up and tell the TRUTH!

"Dearly beloved, we are gathered here! Because last Tuesday, was a happy day for the whole human race! God bless, that Puerto Rican who shot Leroy! Will you look at Leroy? Laid up here, with his eyes closed. Let's not take any chances folks. Keep both hands on your wallet. Until we get this fool in the tomb. I know it is often said, that most people are not really appreciated, until they die. Leroy, you're dead! We appreciate it! But I always try to find something good to say about the dead! Leroy, you're dead! GOOD!!!!!! Can I get a AMEN?

THE TRUTH SHALL MAKE YOU FREE!

Not cute, not rich, or even happy. "You can't handle the truth!" The defendant shouted! (Movie, "A Few Good Men") How many people can really handle the truth? Can you name three individuals in your immediate family, who died and didn't go to heaven? How many people that you really liked, but would admit. They probably didn't make it through the pearly gates? My barber once remarked: "I been going to church for 30 years. I have never heard them preach anyone into hell." And you never will. There are over 1,200 Christian denominations in just the United States alone. Do all of them have time shares reserved in heaven, for each of their members? The Bible book of Genesis covers a period of more than 16 centuries. Enoch, Noah, and Abraham, along with a few family members. They are the only people on earth at that time, to be mentioned by name, as doing God's will. Today there are over 900 million Catholics alone. Nothing can make you instantly happy, the way a lie can. The truth however, is like a knife. A knife so sharp, if you touch the blade with your finger, you could lose a arm. I don't care, tell me the truth and nothing but the truth! As defendants are sworn to do before they testify, and lie. You have to lie, (plead not guilty) or you don't get a trial

I was in court once, when a truly remorseful man wanted to plead guilty to being drunk and disorderly in public. To avoid a mandatory 30 day sentence in jail, the judge persuaded the man to say not guilty. He did, and just walked (staggered) out of the court. The truth did not set him free, a lie did. Don't tell me I'm cute, rich, or skinny. Unless it is the truth! At John 18:37, Pontius Pilate asked Jesus if he is a king? Jesus replied: "For this I have been born, and for this I have come into the world, that I should bear witness to the truth." Pilate said to Jesus: " What is truth?" Then he walked away from Jesus. Noteworthy is that just a few hours before his death, Jesus said: "I have come into the world" (not just to die in sacrifice) "that I should bear witness to the truth" The various essays and topics presented in this book are written in the spirit of the preamble of the United States constitution. "We hold these truths to be, SELF-EVIDENT" It is the sincere desire of the author, with the unbiased authority of the Holy Scriptures, that you will find the TRUTH, that makes you free and happy!

HAPPY MOTHER'S DAY!!!

Of all the holidays celebrated in America, this one confuses me. What is the meaning or the spirit of the occasion. Each year, over one and a half million abortions are performed . World-wide the figure is between 45 to 60 million. They also find dead babies in garbage cans and dumpsters each year. Only the ones they stumble across, make it on the evening news. What about the ones that make it all the way to the landfills? They had a pro-abortion rally in Washington, D. C., and over 300,000 women attended. How many of them were pregnant? None of them! So what's the problem? Less than 1% percent of abortions are the result of rape or incest. What's my point? After my mom marches in a pro-abortion rally, what should I do? Bring her some flowers and candy on Mother's day, and thank her for not exercising her constitutional right to have an abortion? If I were the youngest of five or six kids, I should bring my mom two boxes of candy, and three dozen roses. My mother already had five kids at home, and she walked around for nine months carrying me? If my mom wanted an abortion, would the N. O. W. (National Organization of Women) have picked her up in a limousine, drove her to the abortion clinic, and then treated her to lunch? You think of your mom as a nice person, decent, compassionate, kind, merciful, sympathetic, and pro-choice? Let's not start to argue the issue, that an abortion is right or wrong, a necessary evil etc. If taking steroids, cheating on your income taxes, parking in a handicap zone, are wrong. How can a abortion be right? A bogus repair bill on your automobile is a rip-off. An abortion is not a rip-off? A black congresswoman from Illinois proudly proclaims: "I'm Catholic and pro-choice!" (And God thinks it's Ok) Time soon will tell.

CHAPTER FOUR

A TRUE STORY OF WHAT REAL MOTHERHOOD MEANS!!

This single mom and her six kids were living in the basement of this New York City apartment building. The building caught fire. As the firemen were approaching the building they could see this frantic mother running in and out of the burning basement. By the time she rescued her last baby, the mother's face was so badly burned, she could not open her eyes. She gathered her kids around her, and because she couldn't see them, she used her nose to count and make sure they were all there. This mother was not a woman. It was a cat. A fireman said; "I didn't know a cat could count!" That feline teaches all of us the true meaning of Mother's Day!

MY BIRTH DAY!!

Why do people celebrate a day they don't even remember? If the human life expectancy, was not 70 years, but 70,000 years. Who would pause at the passing of a single calendar year, to have a party? Who celebrates when the odometer on an automobile reaches a 100 miles, or even 10,000. It's too insignificant. I do not celebrate my birthday. However, I remember the day I was born, as if it was yesterday. Of course, the events on the day of my birth were related to me by my mother. I think of her fondly on Mother's day. (Mom, Anna Belle passed away December 24, 1998)

In the words of my mother, as told to me

My mother started having convulsions and fainting spells in her seventh month of pregnancy. By the ninth month, the convulsions were so severe the doctors feared she would die before, or most certainly during delivery. My father signed a document, instructing the doctors, that if only one of us could be saved, they were to save my mom. Anna Belle was only 18 years. (A reasonable decision) The medical conscious and attitude toward abortion was quite different in 1949. So was the technology. In 2005, they would have killed me, and then consoled my mother by telling her they did it to save her life. Besides, she could have more children later. After 14 hours of labor, my mom gave birth to me. She was critical but stable. The doctors did not expect me to live. My grandparents, and a female friend from church, came to the infant intensive care unit. They wanted to spend whatever little time they could, with their first grandchild. Their eyes so full of tears, they could barely see me. The lady friend from church had five kids. Though she was no doctor, to her I didn't look like a baby about to die. I was visually the biggest baby in intensive care. "Skin tight as a watermelon" she later said. I was sucking my thumb so hard, she remarked to my grandparents: "If you don't give that boy a bottle soon, he's going to chew his hand off." That was my birth-day. The rest are not worth celebrating. First the doctors said I wouldn't live, then I would never walk, then I would never talk. (Mom wished the last were true, because I never shut-up) I was born in September 1949, in Holden, West Virginia. Home of those crazy fightin' hillbillies, the Hatfields and Mc Coys. They were too poor to own a trailer, and no trailer park would accept them if they did. So they were just "white trash" Holden was a real one horse town, until the horse ran away. Holden became a "no-horse" town.

FROM BLACK GOAL TO BLACK LUNG

The Island Creek Coal Company, was the the main (only) employer in Holden. They built, stocked, and owned the only grocery store in town. They built and owned the houses, schools, gas stations, roads, everything. Nine out of ten households, had at least one family member, usually the father, who worked in the coal mine. As a child I recall the miners leaving the job at the end of a shift. All of their faces were black from the coal dust. Only if a white miner removed his goggles, the racoon circles around his eyes, revealed he was white. No one had ever heard of OSHA. (Occupation Safety Hazard Administration) If you got fired from the mine, or quit, you were evicted from the house. Whatever money a coal miner earned from Island Creek, within 30 days was back in the company coffers. The house the family rented, the grocery store where they bought food, was all owned by Island Creek Coal Company. If you wrote your name on a dollar bill, you had a good chance of seeing it again. A lot dirtier though. You could spend the same coal dust covered dollar bill several times. You also could get food and gas on credit, if you worked for the mine. Most coal mining families were so far in debt, they owed more money to the company store, than they made each week. Some families were more than a years salary in debt, to the various company owned stores around Holden and Logan West Virginia.

CHAPTER FIVE

Island Creek Coal Company

A popular song on the radio had the lyrics: "Saint Peter don't call me, 'cause I can't go. I owe my soul to the company store." What was the use of of issuing a paycheck with zeros across the front? If you owed more than you had earned. You didn't receive cash. You got company issued script, that could only be redeemed at Island Creek stores. (True story) I did not live that experience. My parents did. Both of my grandfathers died in the coal mine. My mom's dad, when I was only four years old. He was crushed in a ceiling cave-in. My dad's father, at the miraculous age of eighty, from coal dust carcinogens and black lung.. Before he died, he was coughing up flem the size of smurfs, and the color. The coal mine had closed more than 25 years ago. However the hospital wrist-band on my dying grandfather's arm read, Island Creek Coal Company. His name was Cleveland Johnson Sr. (My dad was junior, he had died five years before grandpop. Joe Camel, not the coal mine was the cause of his demise)

Everyone called grandpop Mr. Tom! I never knew why. My father's uncle, (Mr. Tom's baby brother) had moved to New Jersey after getting into a serious fight with one of his brothers. (He bit part of his older brother's top lip, completely off) That was in 1953. After only six months in New Jersey, dad's uncle Arthur had a new car! Everyone thought they were giving away cars up north! So my dad moved the family to Elizabeth, New Jersey. I was 5 years old, my baby sister Bobette was 3 1/2. My dad was a alcoholic as long as I can remember. He was also a wife beater. Sober, he could have easily over-powered my mom. But he only fought when he was drunk, and he was no match. My mom never let me raise my hand to my dad. She didn't need my help.

Domestic violence? My mom was one of eight girls, and they all could fight. I have seen my uncles running down the street being chased by my aunties. Once my uncle Bobby slapped my aunt Daisy. He stayed at our house for a week, before he had the courage to go home. I never saw one of my aunts with a black-eye. I didn't know guys beat-up their wives. I remember watching the O. J. Simpson trial and thinking: " My mother would have killed O. J. so long ago, she would be out of jail by now. O. J. Simpson, had more education, opportunity, and money, than 75% percent of all the White people who ever lived in America. Then he stills winds up in jail. If you can't trust the black men who look like O. J., who can you trust? A good-looking, rich, famous, educated, blackman and he stills turns out to be a wife-batterer? Is O. J. a double-murderer? A better question is: If Nicole Simpson was your sister, would you believe he did it? I didn't kill Ron and Nicole. Everybody I ask says they didn't do it. So if O. J. didn't do it, they must not be dead! No harm, no foul!!

CHAPTER SIX

FROM ALCOHOLISM TO BELIEF IN A "HIGHER POWER"

I had spent Thanksgiving Day at my Aunt Edna's home, along with my mom and other family members. Back at home the next morning, I awoke from a drunken stupor to the sounds of a woman crying. My bed was wet with urine as usual. My mom was unaware of the severity of my alcoholism. I had passed out after dinner at my aunt's house. That was all too familar to my cousins, uncles, and all their friends. With me passed out, my mom sat in horror and deep embarassment, as story after story of my drinking adventures were related. The house was filled with laughter, about my drunk driving arrest, the good jobs lost, the pretty wife that was no more. Someone asked: " Where do you think he will end up? " In jail like the rest of his cousins! After the family and friends had left, and my uncle had gone to bed. My mom and her sister, aunt Edna, talked until late at night about me. I had become unemployable. I had one pair of shoes, hush puppies. I had holes in both soles. On rainy days. I would pay a drinking buddy to go to the liquor store for me. I asked my mom why she was crying? She began to relate some of tales she had heard the previous evening. "Those people have talking about you for years! Why do you go around them? They don't like you!" The tirades from my mom went on for more than a week. I came home drunk every night. I awoke each morning, in a fresh pool of urine. One night I came home early, because I didn't have enough money to get plastered. The covers on my bed were turned back. The sheets were clean and dry. As I lay in the dark, I could hear my mother crying in the next room. She had stayed at my apartment, since following me home Thanksgiving night. After a week, she had seen enough to confirm that all that she had heard was true. Mom yelled: " After what I went through with your father, I will not sit here and watch you drink yourself to death!" She threatened to leave, but she never did. If she had, I know I would have died. Not right away, I was only 33 years old, but sooner or later. My mom used to read the Watchtower magazine. She gave me an article to read, that suggested a way to help alcoholics. A group of doctors, had conducted an experiment on mice.

The Watchtower article entitled: " Those Weaknesses Can Be Overcome" 10/15/1982 page 10 stated: In one experiment, rats were supplied with plain water and water containing alcohol. Some rats drank heavily of the water containing alcohol, others drank only comparatively little, and one rat never drank of it. When the rats were fed a diet especially rich in vitamins and minerals, by and large they greatly decreased their drinking of the water with the alcohol. But when given a diet greatly deficient in essential nutrients, all the rats began drinking large quantities of the water containing alcohol. The experimenters, among whom were some foremost medical researchers, reached the conclusion that there is a definite relationship between the likelihood of alcohol addiction, faulty nutrition.: also that genetic differences accounted for the varying amounts of water containing alcohol, that the various rats drank. (The Watchtower, a cult magazine?)

My mom would cook these delicious meals, but I had no appetite. I began to force myself to eat, and like the mice, the craving for alcohol did not go away. It did lessen to the point I could function. Now I had to deal with reality! No wife, no job, no friends, no money! I was down to a mother's love, that was wearing very thin. She gave me half of the rent money, to keep me from being evicted from my apartment. She gave up her apartment, and moved in with me permanently. Six days after that Thanksgiving Day disaster, I put the "Plug In The Jug!" December 1, 1982 is my dry date. I have never had a drink of alcohol since. That was 23 years ago.

Alcoholics Anonymous motto: " Came to believe that a power greater than ourselves, could restore us to sanity." My mom didn't want me to go to A/A meetings. What if someone sees you? I started going to the meetings, just to have something to do. I promised my counselor I would not drink for 90 days. (I would receive a pin, along with others who completed the 3 months of sobriety) It may seem foolish, but I had disappointed and let down everyone I knew. I didn't want to disappoint this person I barely knew. I realize now, he'd seen dozens of former drunks try and fail. I was so proud to receive my 90 day pin, and shake the hand of my sponsor. I asked my counselor, if he thought God would forgive me for all the bad stuff I had done? Without pausing he said: " God's knows you're an Alcoholic!" and simply walked away. I never spoke to him again, nor can I remember his name. His words, spoken with such conviction remain with me until this day.

My search for the true God did not begin in church. Not in the midst of a group of well dressed Christians, all "Saved" with parking spaces reserved in heaven. It was in a smoked filled room of recovering drunks. (They stop drinking, and smoke even more) My name is Tommy, I'm an Alcoholic. I have not drank in 23 years, because I found the true God, Jehovah. I started reading the Bible everyday. I knew I didn't deserve to go to heaven. I just wanted to know the power, or the person that saved my life.

CHAPTER SEVEN

YOUR AGE IN GOD'S TIME-
ACCORDING TO THE BIBLE

I believe without reservation, that the Bible in it's entirety is the inspired word and will of God. I have read it cover to cover several times. The conclusion I have reached! It is a holy book because it came from God. It is not a book about religion. None of the major religions are mentioned in the Bible. Obviously, none of these churches even existed when the Bible was completed, 2,000 years ago. As often as I read the Bible though, there are just four or five keys scriptures that are truly profound, in what they mean.

Do you know your age in God's time? How can you find out? Read please, 2 Peter 3: 8: " One day is with the Lord as a thousand years, and a thousand years as one day" That simple verse gives an equation of measurement in God's time. 24 hours equals a thousand years. If you divide that equation in half, (24 hours=1,000 years--12 hours=500 years--6 hours=250 years--3 hours=125 years) just three times. What fact becomes apparent? That a 100 year old man, has only existed for 2 hours and 15 minutes in God's time! James 4: 14 is true: "You are a mist, (vapour K. J.) appearing for a little while and then disappearing." So "what is mortal man that you keep him in mind" asked King David. (Psalms 8: 4) I am over fifty years old, and so I ask. If I have existed for only an hour, (fifty years in human time) how could an eternity in hell be justice, for all the bad I have done? Likewise, how many good things could a sinner do in one hour to deserve to go to heaven? Church goers talk about going to heaven, the way kids all want to go to Disneyland. Heaven is some place to go, after you die. From Adam and Eve, to our present day, is less than a week in God's time. What a week it has been! If you think of the Bible as a report card, rather than a religious document. Starting with Adam and Eve, and their lovely first-born Cain. (Profound thought: the first human ever born was a murderer) The conduct of humans for the past 6,000 years includes: Lying, stealing, murder, mass murder, wars, incest, rape, sodomy, bestiality, adultery, fornication, idolatry, child sacrifices etc. All incidents recorded in the Bible. What if the Bible reported about creatures who live on Mars, and not on Earth. Do you think NASA, would have many astronauts volunteering for an exploration of Mars? Hardly! But because we are humans, we excuse the heinous acts committed by mankind. Are we an embarassment to God Almighty? Not at all, in fact he "loved us so much, he gave his son," (John 3: 16) If we were in high school, and the Bible was mankind's report card sent from God our Principal. What grade does the human family earn for itself? For Abraham, "God's friend"--C+. For Noah also a C+, he "walked with God". For Job a C- for his integrity. For King David a D+. For the vast majority of mankind, (90%) straight "F's" across the board. From his vantage point in heaven, Jesus had observed 4,000 years of human conduct. When Jesus came to earth, did he say that any of those billions of humans went to heaven? John 3: 13 says NONE! " No man hath ascended up to heaven" In 4,000 years, nada, zilch, zero!! For-getabout it!

CHAPTER EIGHT

ADAM AND EVE--" YOU WILL POSITIVELY DIE!!"

Words from God Almighty at Genesis 2: 16. Before Adam had a wife, kids, or even built a house. He knew about the death penalty. Adam must have informed his wife, with an additional warning which God had not stipulated: " You must not eat from it, no you must not TOUCH IT!" Eve told the serpent. (Genesis 3:3) After eating of the fruit, both Adam and Eve ran and hid. They were still in the paradise, and they didn't instantly die. But not for long. They were sentenced and evicted on the very day of their breaking a single command from God." No great crime spree! One simple act of disobedience. The judgement? " From dust YOU are, and to dust YOU will return." (Genesis 3:19)

Who was God referring to when he said, "YOU" ? When Adam was standing there naked and ashamed, was he thinking about some life after death, that was going to be better than what he had just lost. Genesis 5; 5 states: " All the days that Adam lived were 930 years and HE died" No where is any distinction made between Adam's body and his soul. After forming Adam from the dust of the ground, and breathing into his nostrils the breath of life. Genesis 2: 7 concludes: " and man BECAME a living soul. He became a living soul, not received a living soul. When someone says : "They put his behind in jail, or the boss fired his behind!" Did just his butt get fired? Only his rear-end went to jail? When God said "YOU", Adam knew he was talking to HIM, body and soul. In every case when you put the word dead, at the end of a sentence. It always means finished, the end. For example:

"Raid--Ant and Roach Spray, "Kills Bugs Dead!"-- "The middle east peace talks are dead!"--"The UPS contract negotiations are dead!"-- "Helen and Dave's marriage is dead!"-- "The car's battery is dead!" Dead means dead! However, when the: "The 102 year old man is dead!" Just his body died? His soul is still alive?. Did Adam believe that? Of course not. If a man who worked for Microsoft was fired by Bill Gates himself. If he was told : "Just your body got fired, your soul still works for Microsoft. Only now instead of getting paid every two weeks. You get all the money you earned after you die!" Who would believe such garbage? The important thing is not what was said to Adam and Eve. But who said it! Yes, God almighty is talking! He didn't mince words when he said: "YOU WILL POSITIVELY DIE!"

What you believe about the dead, is often reflected in how you bury your loved ones. The body of Lazarus was wrapped in bandages, maybe perfumes were applied, and he was placed in a cave. (No thought of life after death) How though, did the Egyptians bury the Pharoahs? In huge pyramids, filled with food, golden treasures, jewelry of all kinds, and even a few unfortunate slaves. Curious however, that none of the Pharoah's EVER sent for the buried treasures. Tomb raiders stole much of it. Why did the Pharoah's not send his slaves to stop them? Ecclesiastes 9: 5 tells us why: " For the living know that they shall die, but the dead know not anything" K. J. There are no dignified dead people! (Not even the Pope) Ecclesiastes 9: 4 says: " A living dog, is better than a dead lion."

The host of a television show named "Crossing Over", claims to be in touch with dead people. If that were true he could make millions with a T. V. show entitled. "Crossing Over-to Find America's Most Wanted". He could solve every homicide in America! (Or the World ?) Who killed Jimmy Hoffa? Who shot JFK? Why Ron Goldman and Nicole Simpson could tell us: Did O. J. do it? It would be too simple. No need for police, and judges, or trial lawyers. No more jury duty! There was an old western movie entitled: " Dead Men Don't Talk" Why would the Mafia put a hit on someone, to keep them from talking? When after the person dies he can get in touch with "Crossing Over" and tell anyway?. They would have to kill the host too! Seriously though, why would God say at Deuteronomy 18: 11, 12 that: "anyone who inquires of the dead...is something detestable (Abomination K. J.) unto the Lord? In the garden of Eden someone was telling a lie. Was it the Devil? "You will positively not die" Or Jehovah God ? When he said: "YOU WILL POSITIVELY DIE!!"

CHAPTER NINE

OMNIPOTENT AND OMNISCIENT-DOES
GOD KNOW EVERYTHING?

A group of junior high school students were asked the question. Where would you go to find the "Sermon on the Mount?" One student answered: "Afghanistan!" That was not the only incorrect answer, but perhaps the most amusing. Too many individuals who consider themselves quite knowledgeable, have a very limted knowledge of a book which claims to be inspired by the wisest Being in the universe. He says at 1 Corinthians 3:19: "For the wisdom of this world is foolishness with God" verse 20 continues: "Jehovah knows that the reasonings of the wise men are futile." In our enlightened modern society, what is the number one topic of interest on the internet? S. E. X.! What industry in America, is larger than MLB, the NFL, and the NBA combined? Pornography! A week ago in God's time, there was no sex. Did you ever hear that the cause of death was, a lack of NOOKY? Did God know in advance, that it would all turn out this way? The Bible shows that nothing can be hidden from God. Concerning two sparrows Jesus said at Matthew 10: 29: "Not one of them will fall to the ground without your father's [knowledge]" Hebrews 4: 13 states: 'There is not a creation that is not manifest to his sight" So God watches pornography? Never!! But nothing escapes his attention. Our Creator, is all-wise. Which simply means he knows more than the entire human race, put together. In fact the same could be said of the angels in heaven, who have existed for billions of years. If God is all-wise, does that mean he knows everything? Is God's entire existence, a continuous series of re-runs, because he already knows the outcome? We also say that God is omnipotent, all powerful. Yet he has given his human and physical creation, some measure of power. The Sun for example, gives off more energy in 60 seconds. Than all the Atomic bombs stockpiled on earth. The mental capacity of God is immearsurable, and truly amazing! Isaiah 40: 26 indicates that God can, "number", "name", and locate, ("not one of them is missing") all the stars in the physical universe. There is only one answer to the series of questions at Isaiah 40: 14. NOBODY!

" With whom did he consult together that one might make him understand, or who teaches him in the path of justice, or teaches him knowledge, of makes him know the very way of real understanding?" Noooooobody!! God has never learned a single thing from one of his creatures, spirit or human. How different it is with human parents. Often a parent may say: "I never thought of that!, or maybe "That's a good idea!", when listening to one of their children. A child that a mother gave birth to, could teach her many things. That is never the case with God. The devil is evil, but also extremely smart. To rebel against God was pretty dumb. However he is still smart enough to be: "misleading the entire inhabited earth", according to Revelation 12: 9 The Devil along with the rest of the angels saw God create the earth. He must know a lot about physics, and even how to make atoms explode. Could he teach humans he is trying to lead to destruction? Certainly! Obviously! Humans have invented more in the last 90 years, than in the previous 6,000. The advance of technology, strangely coincides with the ouster of the Devil from heaven. Is there a pattern, to the madness here on earth?

Again we ask, does God know everything? For example when God asked Abraham to sacrifice his son Isaac. (Genesis 22: 1, 2) He wanted to "tempt" Abraham. That is put him to a test of faith. Was it really a test? Or did God already know the outcome? After the angel stopped Abraham from putting Isaac to death, 22; 12 reads: "for now I do KNOW that you are God fearing." It was only after Abraham passed that test, that God knew for sure, of Abraham's great faith. From then on: "he was called the friend of God." (James 2: 23 K. J.) In the book of Genesis, God pauses six different times after a period of creating and declares: "God saw that it was good." Then he makes a brief over view and declares: "very good!" (Genesis 1: 10, 12, 18, 21, 25, 31) The end of God's creating was the first woman Eve, Adam's wife. By having sexual relations they would carry out God's command: "Be fruitful and multiply, and replenish the earth, and subdue it." A work assignment, that would take thousands of years to accomplish. Looking just at the woman Eve: Did God know in the future there was going to be prostitution? God created women not as physically strong as men. Did he know men would use that superior strength, which God gave them to rape and abuse women? Did he already know there was going to be incest, sexual abuse, child molesters, pedaphiles, pornography, abortions, child sacrifices, etc.? IMPOSSIBLE! Why? Because what he had just made was, "very good". When the Israelites burned their children in sacrifices, to demonic God's. Jeremiah 7: 31 says: " which I cammanded them not, neither came it into my heart." God did not command it! The evil act never crossed his mind. God is not the author, or promoter, of all the wicked actions of humans under the influence of demons. Psalms 106: 37 states: "yea, they sacrificed their sons and their daughters unto devils." Deuteronomy 32: 4 says of God: "The rock, perfect is his activity, For ALL his ways are justice." But verse five says of humankind: 'They have acted ruinously on their own part; They are not his children, the defect is their own" There is no scripture that says: "We are all God's children!" However 1 John 3: 7 does say: "Little children, let no one mislead you; he who carries on righteousness is righteous."

1 John 3: 8 continues; "He who carries on sin originates with the Devil" Verse ten concludes: "The children of God and the children of the Devil are evident by this fact; Everyone who does not carry on righteousness does not originate with God."

Jehovah, does not need to know everything to be our God. Starting with Adam and Eve, humans have refused to be taught by God. So if humans do not listen to their creator, what benefit is there for God to know everything? People admire someone who is called a genius. They seek advice, try to "pick their brains", so to speak. Some of the same people who say "God knows everything", don't listen to God or seek his advice. If they did the words of Isaiah 54: 13 would come true.

"And all thy children shall be taught of the Lord; and great shall be the peace of thy children."

CHAPTER TEN

GOD WORKS IN MYSTERIOUS WAYS !!

The above often repeated expression, is found nowhere in the Bible. Nor is; "God helps those who help themselves." God helps those who do his will!! 1 John 2: 17 promises: "he that does the will of God remains forever." To those who claimed to be doing God's will, ("did we not prophesy, expel demons, do powerful works, in your name?") Jesus replied: "Get away from me, you workers of lawlessness." Matthew 7: 21-23. Let's take a look at some of the mysterious ways of God, when tragedy strikes!

Pearl Harbor, Oklahoma City, Hiroshima, or when that lady in Texas was drowning her five kids! Where was God? What was he doing? Did he see all of these events? Yes, if he chose to. Could he have stopped them all? (With the blink of a eye) Then why didn't he? (It was not his will to intervene) That is obvious, not mysterious! Where were the invisible rescuers for humans, the angels? Spirit creatures had existed in heaven, for billions of years, before the creation of man. Were they all just sitting around bored with nothing to do? Then one day God appointed them, "guardian angels"! Now the angels had a purpose? Ridiculous! The truth is that the angels work for God, not humans. Daniel 7: 10 describes at least 100 million spirit creatures, "ministering to the ancient of day's" At Luke 13:4, a tower fell killing 18 people. (World Trade Center) Jesus spoke of them as being no worse debtors, than all other men inhabiting Jerusalem. Wrong place, wrong time, no guardian angels. No mysterious ways of God. One of the most difficult notions for humans to fathom is this. Our Creator was busy, happy, productively occupied, and absolutely self-content, for trillions of years. Then he decided to create humans. For obedient humans, life would be problem free. They would never need the help of the "guardian angels". Likewise, God created no invisible safety net for humans, who deliberately made a practice of disobeying him. God's familiar words at John 3:16; "God love the world so much...he gave his only begotten son."

That verse is the answer to the simple question. Why did God not just destroy all humans, a thousand years ago? Or at least a hundred years ago! There would have been no World Wars, no holocaust, no Rwanda, no Spanish influenza, no A.i.d.s., the list is endless. How does God love mankind? By allowing the offspring of wicked people to be born at all! How does God show he cares? By having in place, a solution to all the problems humans have brought upon themselves. Believing they were ruling themselves. But in reality being mislead by the Devil. (Revelation 12: 9) God has allowed nothing to happen on this earth, that he cannot erase, reverse, or restore.

Well, when will he begin the process? When he is good and darn ready!! Daniel 4: 35 reminds all mankind: "All the inhabitants of the earth are being considered as merely nothing, and he is doing his OWN WILL among the army [angels] of the heavens, and the inhabitants of the earth. AND THERE EXIST NO ONE THAT CAN CHECK HIS HAND OR THAT CAN SAY TO HIM, "WHAT HAVE YOU BEEN DOING?" That is not mysterious, it is obvious! Can you handle the truth??

CHAPTER ELEVEN

THE HIGHLY INFECTIOUS--CHURCH BRAIN SYNDROME

CHURCH BRAIN: definition; a common malady among regular church goers; It can cause an individual to accept as true, teaching or beliefs, that apply only in church. But nowhere else in the persons daily life experience.

The following questions are not for the purpose of changing beliefs or thinking. It is not a test. There is no passing or failing grade based on your answers. However, honesty and consistency in your answers will perhaps reveal. Whether what you believe in your HEART, is in harmony with what you think in your MIND.

LUKE 10:27

"Thou shalt love the Lord thy God with all thy HEART...and with all thy MIND"

PLEASE TAKE THE FOLLOWING QUIZ

1.   2 Peter 3: 8 says: "One day with Lord is as a thousand years"

True_____ False_____

2.   Humans have existed for less than a week in God's time

True_____ False_____

3.　　God has seen mankind, rob, rape, and murder each other

True_____ False_____

4.　　Genesis to Malachi covers nearly 4,000 years of human history

True_____ False_____

5.　　Then God came to earth, and let humans he created, kill him?

True_____ False_____

Matthew 26 : 67 says: "They spit into his face, and hit him with their fist, others slapped him in the face."

6.　　A father wants love, respect, and obedience from his children

True_____ False_____

7.　　Will children love, respect, and obey a parent they spit upon?

Yes_____ No _____

8.　　Did you ever spit on your parents?

Yes_____ No _____

9.　　Would you allow your children to spit on you?
Yes_____ No _____

10.　　Do you believe in your HEART, that God let humans do that to him?

Yes_____ No _____

11.　　But at least in your MIND, do you wonder if that is true?

Yes_____ No _____

12.   Have any of the angels in heaven ever spit on God?

Yes_____ No _____

Selfishness definition; When you believe in your heart, that someone should do for YOU, what you would not even THINK, of doing for them.

13.   Before God would come to earth, and let humans he created a week ago kill him.He would send the angels to kill all six billion of us.

True_____ False_____

14.   God Cannot Lie! (Hebrews 6: 18) God cannot DIE! (Psalms 36: 9)

True_____ False_____

15.   Are the words Easter, Christmas, Or Trinity in the Bible?

Yes_____ No _____

16.   Would you open a Trinity checking account? 3 dollars=1 dollar

Yes_____ No _____

Answers: (from author) 1. True 2. True 3. True 4. True 5. False 6. True 7. NO 8. NO 9. NO 10. NO 11. NO 12. NO 13. True 14. True 15. NO 16. NO

Thank you for your time, and honest answers!

CHAPTER TWELVE

WHEN GOD KILLS--IT IS NOT MURDER

Exodus 20: 13 states simply: "You must not murder!" That commandment along with nine others, are requirements for one who claims to love God. Also, a repeated practicer of even one of these prohibitions, would make his worship unacceptable. Clearly, because life comes from God, a human who kills is sinning. But not just against his fellowman. An even greater sin is committed, against the "source of life!" himself.

Psalms 36: 9 says: "with you is the source of life!" God does not have life. HE IS LIFE!! Life has always existed, because God had no creator. Humans, plants, animals, and the spirit creatures in heaven, were all created first. Then given life from God himself. Therefore, how dare you snuff out of existence, something that came from God? It is MURDER!! Our righteous, and supremely holy Creator, never lies, steals, or commits adultery. He obeys his own laws, and certainly humans to the best of their ability should do the same. What if his creatures deliberately, and repeatedly disobey?

Does the commandment, "thou shall not murder", apply to God. NO IT DOES NOT! Life is a gift! (Romans 6: 23) God reserves the right, to at any time take back that life he gave as a gift. The gift came not from your parents, but from your Creator. Your parents, by pro-creation, pass along the life they have received. (Pro-choice people don't seem to see that abortion is unfair, besides murder) So, it is not murder, for God to destroy disobedient humans. A boss has the right to fire, an employee. Does not the "Boss" of the universe, have the same right? How many humans were destroyed by God in the entire Bible account? I don't know! Here are a few examples

Add up the total number of persons destroyed by God in these Bible accounts;

Leviticus 10: 1 (2)--Numbers 16: 49 (14,700)--Numbers 25: 9 (24,000)

1 Samuel 16: 19 (50,000)--2 Samuel 24: 15 (70,000) 2 Kings 19: 35 (185,000)

Numbers 15: 32 (1)--2 Kings 2: 24 (42 "little children" K. J.) Total=373,745

These eight accounts do not include the flood of Noah's day! Then you read the prophecy of Jeremiah 25: 33 concerning a future "DAY" when: "those slain by the Lord shall be at that day from one end of the earth even unto the other end of the earth; they shall not be lamented, neither gathered, nor buried, they shall be dung upon the ground"

GOD KILLS HUMANS! HUMANS DO NOT KILL GOD! WHY NOT?

BECAUSE THAT WOULD BE MURDER!

CHAPTER THIRTEEN

IS THERE ONE TRUE RELIGION? HOW CAN YOU FIND IT?

D o you really want to find it? Could you handle the truth, if you found it?

If you carried the gene for alzheimer's. Would you want to know now? Does it really matter, you will find out the truth sooner or later. I often hear people say: "I have my own religion, I'm very strong in my beliefs" Did they reach that conclusion after an exhaustive study of the Bible, or personal research? People often become defensive, or even offended when you question what they believe. Emotions become involved.

Yes, there is an emotional attachment to long held convictions. Who wants to be told, "You paid way too much for that plasma TV!" No one. "Look here at this newspaper ad. You paid 1,800 dollars, but the same television is on sale for $1,200" No I don't want to see it! Fear, embarassment, pride, anger, are all natural feelings. We've all been there. Many have the same feelings, when it comes to religion. However as I stated earlier, the Bible is not a book about religion. It is a book of TRUTH! Jesus said at John 17: 17: "thy word is truth". How many versions of the truth can there be? If there is only one version, which is the original? How can you be sure? Here's one way!

THE DEVIL KNOWS THE TRUE RELIGION

If only we could capture the Devil, put him in a strait-jacket, and force him to drink truth serum. I wonder what denomination he would name? The Devil must know. He has been around longer, than any religion on earth. Having been in the very presence of God himself. He is fully aware of the one true faith, but he doesn't want anyone to find it. So why not start or influence, not just one false way of worship, but dozens? Or perhaps hundreds? Finding the TRUE religion, would be like finding a needle in a haystack. The "father of the lie", does not want you to find the TRUE religion. (John 8: 44) But he knows which one it is! Perhaps the key is, not to find a church that you like. But rather, find the church that the Devil does not like. Yes, find the religion that the Devil hates! Acts 28: 22 says: "concerning this sect, we know that Every Where it is spoken against!" So how could the true religion, be a very large, popular, highly respected, well spoken of church or organization?

JESUS ALSO KNOWS THE TRUE RELIGION

But he wants you to find it! However, Jesus himself said at Matthew 7: 13, 14: "MANY would be on the road to destruction, but FEW would [even] find the narrow way leading to life" What does that illustration mean? That the majority of people are on the road to destruction. Clear and simple! That should not discourage you. It just means you have to be careful. Very careful! A powerful invisible person is out to mislead you. If there are a thousand different churches in America alone. Then the MAJORITY, are on the road to destruction. Final answer! Jesus gave other clues. Matthew 7: 16, 17 states:'Ye shall know them by their fruits....a corrupt tree bringeth forth evil fruit."

MY WHOLE FAMILY IS "SAVED"!

I am always amazed by such statements. Note Jesus words at Matthew 10: 36: "a man's foes shall be they of his own household" Verse 21 says: "The brother shall deliver up the brother to death, and the father the child, the children shall rise up against their parents, and cause them to be put to death" Verse 22 concludes: Ye shall be hated of all men for my name's sake" So if your whole family is "Saved", could ALL of you perhaps be on the road to destruction? Or is Jesus mistaken in just your family's case? Be careful!

CHAPTER FOURTEEN

JESUS CHRIST, MY PERSONAL SAVIOR

I was once asked by a co-worker: "Would you like to accept Jesus, as your personal savior? It's easy!" (He was smoking a Marlboro, while holding a Bible. He died a year later from a heart attack. He hated the Watchtower magazine, but he was "Saved") I have a personal trainer at the gym. My personal physician, my personal accountant, etc. They all work for me, and I pay them. In what sense is Jesus a personal savior? I could not find that expression anywhere in scripture.

I read that the mass murderer, Ted Bundy, had also accepted Jesus as his personal savior. This was just prior to his being executed in Florida. I asked a born again Christian if he really believed, Mr. Bundy was in heaven? He replied: "Yes!!" Very emphatically, and not appreciating the incredulous tone in my voice. I told him: "Perhaps a few of those poor women, could also have been "Saved". But their lives were cut short, by a man who's now in heaven, hob-knobbing with Jesus?" My personal savior, just sounds too subservient to me. Jesus Christ was the greatest man who EVER lived. Though now in heaven, he is still the greatest man who EVER lived. He will ALWAYS be, the greatest man who EVER lived

Jesus did not say it would be easy to gain salvation. " The Son of man must suffer many things...and be slain" (Luke 9: 22) "If any man come after me, let him deny himself, and take up HIS cross daily" Verse 23 concludes. Jesus never spoke of being anyones personal savior. Nor was salvation assured, and already guaranteed. Rather, Matthew 24: 9 warns against over confidence: "But he that has endured to the end is the one that will BE SAVED." The end of your life in faithfulness, or the end of this wicked world, which ever comes first. " Oh, I got saved in 1992!" Not according to Jesus words! Also, what part of being persecuted, or even being killed was going to be easy? Compromising is easy. Standing firm for the truth, may cost you your life.

CHAPTER FIFTEEN

HEIL HITLER--OR DIE!! WHICH CHURCHES REFUSED?

A professor of history, John Weiss, wrote a book entitled: "Idealogy of Death". He compared public statements from the major religions during the reign of Nazi Germany: " In 1934 the Evangelical church insisted the Nazis must be 'welcomed by Lutheranism' and thanked 'the Lord God' for giving the Germans a 'pious and trusty overlord'.... A Protestant bishop wrote to his clergy, [Hitler] "has been sent to us by God" Weiss continues:"The German Methodist church...agreed with Bishop Dibelius that Hitler had saved Germany from an imminent Bolshevik revolution...

"bringing peace and stability .... The Mormon church advised it's faithful that opposing Hitler was a violation of Mormon law" and he adds: Catholics were told it was a sacred duty to obey the new state, a duty never withdrawn even after the full horrors in the east were known to the clergy. Did any Christians oppose Hitler? Professor Weiss states: " as a group, only the Jehovah's Witnesses resisted the Nazis." Continues Professor Weiss: "yet any witness sent to a concentration camp could have been released by signing a paper, renouncing his or her faith." A Protestant pastor wrote of them, "not the great churches, but these slandered and scoffed at people were the ones who stood up first against the rage of the Nazi demon, and who dared to make opposition according to their faith." (Amazing conduct for a cult, would you agree?)

CHAPTER SIXTEEN

MODERN CHURCH TEACHINGS

What do Santa Claus, the Easter bunny, and the Trinity, have in common? None of them are mentioned in the Bible. No problem, say many Trinitarians! No problem? How could you claim to believe that Lazarus, and others were raised from the dead? If the word resurrection, was not in the Bible. The same is true for words like, rapture, purgatory, and limbo. The Bible had some forty writers, over a period of sixteen centuries. Written under the influence of the Holy Spirit. (One third of the so-called Trinity) Can you prove that any of those men EVER, spoke of, knew of, or even heard of the word Trinity? How can you write about the Holy Spirit, and not about the Trinity? If the Holy Spirit is part of the Trinity?

Jesus, who is also part of the so-called Trinity. Never uttered the word Trinity. The apostles themselves, did not believe, nor were they taught that Jesus was God, in the flesh. So why is the Apostle John's inspired book, the most often quoted by supporters of the Trinity? Prove the apostle John ever heard the word, Trinity! What is the Greek word for Trinity? When was the term coined? Long after the Apostle John's death. The book of Revelation, completed in 96 C.E. states at chapter one verse one: " The Revelation of Jesus Christ, which GOD gave unto him." The Apostle John wrote the book of Revelation. Two years later in his book of John, he wrote quoting Jesus: "for my father is greater than I am." (John 14: 28) Then after his ressurection Jesus said: "I ascend unto MY father, and your father; and to MY God, and your God." (John 20:17)

What about John 1: 1." the word was God" K.J. But some translations say for example: "and the word was a god" (1808 The New Testament in an improved Version)

"and the word was divine" (1935 The Bible-An American Translation)

" and the Word was a God" (1958 The New Testament, by James L. Tomanek

"and a God (or, of a divine kind) was the word" (1975 Das Evangelium nach Johannes, by Johannes Schneider) We have learned more about the Greek language since 1611, when the King James version was written. Almost 400 years ago.

Notice what the apostle Paul wrote as the salutation, for three of his inspired books. All from the King James version: 2 Corinthians 1: 3 "blessed be God, even the father of our Lord Jesus Christ." At Ephesians 1:3 it says: "Blessed be the God and the father of our Lord Jesus Christ." And again at 1 Peter 1:3" Blessed be the God and the Father of our Lord Jesus Christ." All three of those Bible books were written, after the resurrection of Jesus to Heaven. " Therefore being at the right hand of God" Acts 2: 33

The Bible speaks for itself. There is no mystery! John 1: 1 is not the heaviest scripture in the Bible. Unless you just want to believe in the Trinity. Also there may be some Christian pastors, you admire and respect. There is an emotional attachment also. However after examining the facts, and listening to both sides of the issue. The Trinity is to many Christians, what evolution is to a astro-physicist. The scientist may proclaim his absolute faith in evolution. However, when he opens his garage door Monday morning, and his brand new car is missing. When he calls the police to report that his car is taken, he makes this bold assertion: "Somebody, stole my car!" He didn't see anyone take the car. He didn't hear the car drive away. How can he be so positive that someone took his automobile? If the scientist was told, that one of the avenues the detectives were pursuing. Is the possibility, that his brand new Lexus evolved out of his garage. How? Well it's just a theory, but here goes......Perhaps the garage door was struck by lightening, causing his automatic door to open...then static electricity caused the car's ignition to start by itself...Then a jolt of thunder caused the transmission to fall into reverse....Then when the rear tires struck the curb, the transmission moved into drive... Then somehow the car drove itself away! That astro-physicist would be insulted by the mere suggestion of such a preposterous theory! That story is million times more likely, then for even one human cell, to have evolved by itself. Evolution is a lie, and a insult to God. So likewise is the Trinity, Santa Claus, and the Easter bunny!

CHAPTER SEVENTEEN

ONLY "GOD THE FATHER"

There is not a single reference to either, God the Son, or God the Holy Spirit, in the sacred scriptures. Here is just a partial list of the many times the Bibles speaks of: "Only God the Father" (All King James Version)

Galations 1:3: "Grace be to you and peace from GOD THE FATHER"

Philippians 1: 2 "Grace be unto you, and peace, from GOD OUR FATHER"

1 Thessalonians 1:1 "the church of the Thessalonians...is in GOD THE FATHER"

"and peace from GOD OUR FATHER, and the lord Jesus Christ"

2 Timothy 2: 2 "and peace, from GOD THE FATHER and Christ Jesus our Lord"

No interpretation needed! God's word speaks for itself. 1 Corinthians 8: 6 says: "But to us there is but one GOD, THE FATHER...and one Lord Jesus Christ.." Note, no mention of the Holy Spirit. If a Martian landed on earth, and he was handed a Bible.

After reading the Bible from cover to cover. The Martian is asked; "Who was Jesus Christ?" He would simply answer: "The son of God!" Which is the same answer Peter gave when Jesus asked him at Matthew 16:15, 16: " But whom say ye that I am?...Thou art the Christ, the Son of the living God." Did Jesus correct Peter's answer? Or add to it "Peter, I'm also God in the flesh, as in the Trinity!" No because the disciple's answer was simple and correct, and not a mystery. It was the TRUTH!

CHAPTER EIGHTEEN

SATAN THE DEVIL--A PATHOLOGICAL LIAR

A good enough liar to mislead: "the entire inhabited earth" (Revelation 12: 9) The Devil has lied to humans for thousands of years. From the time we are born we begin to take in information. Is all of it true? Have you spent 20, 30, 40 years or more on this earth, without running into even one of the Devil's lies? Is that possible? Have you ever met an Adult, who had never had a cold? Ever met a parent who's child, never had the flu? Would you believe it, if they said it? No! There are too many sick people, and too many germs around to catch, or come in contact with. The Devil started telling lies, before any human ever had a sore throat, or the flu. The lies of Satan are more contagious, and pervasive than the common cold. Those lies have been repeated, so often and for so long. They are now accepted as true, without question. That is why you must "search for the true God.". Because: "the God of this world hath blinded the minds" (2 Corinthians 4:4), of most of mankind today. By infecting our ancestors with lies, we got it from them.

It is hard for people living in our modern times, to imagine that people 500 years ago believed, the earth was flat. That was the scientific fact of the times. Nearly everyone believed it, but it was wrong. The astronomer Galileo, was nearly killed for saying the earth revolved around the Sun. The fact that the majority of mankind believed it, did not make it true. In Fact you would expect the truth to be, "controversial"! The whole world is under the influence of Satan. 'The father of the LIE" John 8: 44

Contrary to public opinion, and all the scientific knowledge available in 1492. The Bible accurately stated, that the earth was not flat. Not supported on the back of some mythical man, Atlas. 2,000 years before Columbus boarded his ship. A humble farmer named Job wrote: "He stretcheth out the North over the empty place, and hangeth the earth upon NOTHING" (Job 26: 7) Where did Job get that information? This was 1,400 years before Jesus came to earth. But even more amazing, is what Isaiah wrote 700 years after Job. Isaiah 40: 26 proclaims: "It is he that sitteth upon the CIRCLE of the earth." Where did Job and Isaiah get accurate, factual information, that even the scientific community did not possess? Nor could it be proven! No telecopes, no pictures, no space shuttle. It was accurate and true. But not what the majority believed.

CHAPTER NINETEEN

WHAT ARE THE LIES--OF THE MASTER SLANDERER?

"Good Teacher, by doing what shall I inherit everlasting life?" Jesus said to him: "Why do you call me good.?" "Nobody is good except one, GOD" (Note: Only One is good, not three. Plus Jesus says it wasn't him. If Jesus is God, he is lying to this man.)

According to popular opinion, The Trinity, Hellfire, and the Immortal soul, are true. Those three doctrines are shared by 98% of all the Christian denominations on earth. Even non-Christian religions, such as Hindu, and Buddhism have similar teachings. Are those three religious tenets true? If more than five billion people on earth, have been taught the truth. Who is the Devil misleading? The majority of humans have out-smarted the, "father of the Lie"! Bravo to humanity! I have a question: " How do you squeeze all those billions of people, onto the "narrow way"? (Matthew 7: 13) The road to destruction is supposed to be crowded, not the road to life.

The largest Christian television network is named, the Trinity Broadcast Network. Why pick a word that is not even in the Bible, to identify a Christian television station? Why would the Devil allow that "Truth", to be proclaimed 24 hours a day? If TBN is leading people to the truth, why is it not: "spoken against every where"? (Acts 28: 22) The Watchtower, (Published by Jehovah's Witnesses) is the only magazine on earth that has the name of God, Jehovah on the cover. 52 million times a month, in nearly 200 different languages. Even if nobody reads the Watchtower, and it's just a waste of paper. 200 languages a month is an amazing feat, for a cult. For a prize of two front row seats in heaven: Name 75 languages!! How about 50 languages? Same prize!!

The Watchtower from it's inception in 1879. Has always rejected, the Trinity, Hellfire, and the Immortal Soul. Plus everywhere I go, the Watchtower is "spoken against"! I wish I could ask the Devil who he hates! The Trinity Broadcast Network, or the Watchtower? Someone find the truth serum, please!

If the Trinity, Hellfire, and the Immortal soul are true. Then name three lies of Satan the Devil. Then show me all the people he is leading to destruction. According to Revelation 12: 9 he is "misleading the entire inhabitated earth" Who are they, and where are they all at? There are not enough Jehovah's Witnesses on earth, to mislead the state of California. They are the only church that says the "earth is not flat". Who's right? I don't think The Devil likes Jehovah's Witnesses. A whole lot of Christians don't either! There are just too many people clapping, singing, and shouting Hallelujah. To fit on the "narrow way". Final note; According to the Random House College Dictionary-Revised Edition: Word: Hallelujah. Definition: Hebrew Halleluyah; "Praise ye Jehovah"!

CHAPTER TWENTY

THE RESURRECTION-RIGHTEOUS
AND UNRIGHTEOUS PEOPLE

"There shall be a resurection of the dead, both the just and the unjust." (Acts 24: 15 K.J.) The disciple Luke spoke of the resurrestion, as a future event. When everyone of the billions of people, who have ever lived on this earth. Will have two opportunities to be resurrected. Preferably as a righteous person. But if it gets you out of the grave, even the unrighteous tag will do. Not just one chance, all or nothing. Two chances to live again on earth. Not heaven, here on earth. You died on earth, what's so unfair about being brought back to earth? Psalms 37: 29 states: "The righteous themselves will possess the earth, and they will reside FOREVER upon it." Which makes perfect sense, according to Isaiah 45: 18 "God himself that formed the earth and made it... he created it not in vain, he formed it to be inhabitated." The resurrection of righteous men such as Abraham, his son Isaac, and his grandson Jacob are guaranteed. So much so, that God viewed them as already alive, over 1,900 years ago. Luke 20: 38 says: "He is a God, not of the dead, but of the living, for they are all living TO HIM." Though they remain asleep in death to this very day. But worry not, "for the hour is coming, in which all that are in the graves shall hear his voice, and shall come forth" (John 5: 28) Not that dead persons can hear voices. For the benefit of the living eye witnesses, Jesus cried with a loud voice: "Lazarus, come forth. And he that was dead came forth." (John 11: 43, 44) It is interesting, that Lazarus did not speak of seeing anyone. Not even Abraham, in whose "bosom" he was in for 4 days. (Luke 16: 23) There was nothing to tell, because he had no memory.

Death is like a sleep, with no dreams. The brain is dead, so how can you dream? The perfect memory of a loving and forgiving God, is the safest place for those billions who have died here on earth.

I was watching a PBS program. (Public Broadcast Station) It dealt with the horrors and evils of slavery. "Sharks used to follow the slave ships, as they sailed from Africa." Said the narrator. I cringed in the hope that those poor individuals, were already dead. When they were thrown overboard to be quickly eaten. All is not lost, that slave has two chances of living here on earth again. By being resurrected, as a righteous or unrighteous person. For the resurrection to be just and unbiased, it has to be administered by God himself, or someone he appointed. We have no idea who those poor Africans were. What if humans were in charge of who gets resurrected, or not? Complaints of neglect, bias, prejudice, nationalism, favoritism, racism, or just oops!, we never heard of you! " What was your name? You were eaten by a shark.?" Plantation owners like Thomas Jefferson, would be resurrected. While many of the slaves he owned, would remain in an anonymous grave. Not remembered, or even missed. However Jesus promised that: "ALL THOSE in the memorial tombs will hear his voice, and come out." (John 5: 28) No one left behind. No rich powerful people first, and poor people last. We must wait to see how Matthew 19: 30 is fulfilled: "But many that are first will be last, and the last first." The resurrection will be fair, because God is Just!

CHAPTER TWENTY ONE

TWELVE STEPS--IN MY SEARCH FOR THE TRUE GOD

I sat in the smoke filled basement of a church, waiting for the Alcoholics Anonymous meeting to begin. I noticed a book on a table, it was blue. It was entitled: "Twelve Steps and Twelve Traditions" I knew twelve was a significant number in the Bible. There were 12 tribes in Israel. Jesus chose 12 apostles. When Judas turned traitor, and later died. Matthias was chosen to replace Judas Iscariot. He becoming the 12th apostle. (Acts 1: 26). I knew of the "big blue book", Alcoholics Anonymous! But what were these twelve steps and traditions? I asked to borrow the "step" book, since I could not afford to buy my personal copy. I had one pair of shoes, hush puppies. They had holes in both soles. I hated going to the liquor store on rainy days. It sometimes took 48 hours or more, for my shoes to completely dry-out. I had not drank in 60 days. (90 days of sobriety, you receive a pin) That was an amazing feat for someone, who drank orange juice every morning. Laced with Vodka. Well the first glass of O. J., was with bacon and eggs. The second glass was with vodka. By 11 am. everyday I at least had a "buzz", (a high). I would meet a friend for lunch, say "Hellooo." " My goodness Tommy! Have you been drinking already?" I didn't think it was strange to have alcohol on my breath, at 10 am. in the morning. Nor was standing in line waiting for the liquor store to open, a sign that I had a serious drinking problem. It was like going to the bank. Before the liquor store manager could put the cash in the register, I wanted my Vodka. I just wanted a drink so early in the morning. I didn't need it! Those poor wino's waiting behind me on line, had a drinking problem. The store manager would make change out of a paper bag, until the line was gone. No time even to put the cash in the register drawers. I did not think my conduct was strange. Denial, is not a river in Egypt!

CAME TO BELIEVE THAT A POWER GREATER THAN OURSELVES

COULD RESTORE US TO SANITY (Step two) 12 Steps and 12 traditions

I would not be alive today, if I had not come in contact with Alcoholics Anonymous. A/A saved my life. The Bible, how to live my life sober. I personally believe, that the same "higher power" that inspired the Bible. Also inspired some parts, or statements in the twelve step book. I sincerely believe that! I try to read the Bible everyday. On the anniversary of my dry date each year, December 1, 1982. I reread the Twelve steps and Twelve traditions book. 23 years, one day at a time. During the early days of my sobriety, I would read the "12 steps" everyday. At certain passages, I would ask myself: "Who is talking?" It can't be a human author, can it? Here are a few examples of [I believe] God speaking in the Twelve step book.

[Page 25 Next to last sentence] " How he does cherish the thought that man, risen so majestically from a single cell in the primordial ooze, is the spearhead of evolution and therefore the only God that his universe knows!" Words of contempt from God himself!

[Page 29] "scientific progress told us there was nothing man couldn't do. Knowledge was all-powerful. Intellect could conquer nature." Who's words?

[Page 70 Last paragraph] "With great intelligence, men of science have been forcing nature to disclose her secrets. The immense resources now being harnessed, promise such a quantity of material blessings, that many believe that a man-made millennium lies just ahead. Poverty will disappear, and there will be such abundance that everybody can have all the security and personal satsifactions he desires. The theory seems to be that once everbody's primary instincts are satisfied, there won't be much left to quarrel about. The world will then turn happy and be free to concentrate on culture and character. Soley by their own intelligence and labor, men will have shaped their own destiny." Positively inspired, I sincerely believe!!!

[72 Second paragraph]" For just as long as we were convinced, that we could live exclusively by our own individual strength and intelligence, for just that long was a working faith in a higher power impossible. We could actually have earnest religious beliefs which remained barren because we were still trying to play God ourselves. As long as we placed self-reliance first, a genuine reliance upon a higher power was out of the question. That basic ingredient of all humility, a desire to seek and do God's will was missing" No human, could speak to another human, that way.

[Page 32 bottom third] " In no deep or meaningful sense had we EVER taken stock of ourselves, made amends to those we had harmed, or freely given to ANY human being without demand for reward. We had not even prayed rightly. We had always said: "Grant me my wishes" instead of "Thy will be done". The love of God and man we understood not at all. Therefore we remained self-deceived." A thump on my hard-head!!

[Page 75 second paragraph] " During this process of learning more about humility, the most profound result of all was the change in our attitude toward God. We began to get over the idea that the Higher Power was a sort of bush-league pinch hitter to be called upon only in an emergency. Many of us who thought ourselves religious awoke to the limitations of this attitude. Refusing to put God first, we had deprived ourselves of his help." Who could describe my situation, as if he was there?

Those few excerpts, and many more I would read everyday. Still in a mental fog, I asked myself: "Were these the words of Bill W.? (Co-founder Alcoholics Anonymous) The wisdom of the Twelve steps, far surpasses that of any human alone. The Higher Power had to have a name. There must be a purpose to life, beyond temporary pleasures. Most of all, I wanted to know the person who saved my life. I said a prayer: "Lord, if you help me. I promise to show the same zeal for doing right, as I had for doing wrong." I began to SEARCH for the true God. " If you SEARCH for him he will let himself be found by you." (1 Chronicles 28: 9)

CHAPTER TWENTY TWO

WHO CARES? "WHEN THE SAINTS COME MARCHING IN"?

After spending a weekend in New Orleans for my family reunion, I boarded a plane for Chicago. I remember thinking, if I never hear; "when the saints come marching in" again. It will be too soon! Marching into where, heaven? What would the angels be doing while we "strut our stuff"? Stomping their feet and clapping, waving palm branches, standing and cheering the chorus? The lyrics and the thinking behind the song are ridiculous. Here's why! At Job 38: 4 God asked: Where did you happen to be when I founded the earth?" Not only Job, but the entire human race did not exist. Nor would humans be created for another several Billion years. However in heaven, intelligent spirit creatures that already existed: "all the sons of God, began shouting in applause." Job 38: 7

If the universe is ten to fifteen billion years old as some physicist estimate. Then the angels in heaven are at least that old. Probably, even much older. Intelligent creatures, think, compose, build, write, create, laugh, sing, and LEARN. How much knowledge would a 15 billion year old human have? What about a spirit creature, that never needed sleep? The expression: "I have forgotten more things than you know". Would certainly apply in comparison to what an angel must know, versus a frail imperfect human. What could a mortal human being, possibly add to the knowledge, or life experience of any heavenly creature? We all understand, what the word senority means. "I was working here for 30 years, when you walked through the door!"

Can you imagine a newly hired assembly-line worker, "marching" into General Motors? Would all the assembly lines in America, stop and admire this employee with zero senority? Some born again Christians seem to think, that experience is awaiting them in heaven. A big white float, with them riding down "Jesus Avenue". All the angels waving and throwing confetti. When Billy Graham gets to heaven, will" all the sons of God [begin] shouting in applause"? I truly doubt it!. "Let's all give a round of applause to this puny, sinful human born on earth a hour ago.!" Please stand while he comes "Marching In!" When Paul and Jan Crouch get to heaven, almighty God himself will be standing and cheering. Seriously though, you have to be terribly self-deceived or misled to think. Perfect creatures in heaven, are waiting for a bunch of "sinners" to come "marching In". What, no senority position will be waiting for you? Mopping the floors, or cleaning the angels locker room? Absurd. Psalm 115: 16 states: "As regards the heavens, to Jehovah the heavens belong, but the earth he has given to the sons of men." Oh, by the way. 'The whole earth belongs to me [too]" Exodus 19: 5

CHAPTER TWENTY THREE

COME ON EVERYBODY! LET'S PLAY JEOPARDY!!

FAMOUS AMERICANS-JEOPARDY

CATERGORY--NONE OF THEM

$100 Answer: Left eye, (Lisa Lopes) Tupac Shakur, Biggie Small, Alliyah

Question: Which of these R&B singers are in heaven?

$200 Answer: George Washington, Thomas Jefferson, Abraham Lincoln

Question: How many of the founding fathers are in heaven?

$300 Answer: Tom Landry, Pat Tillman, Walter Payton, Reggie White

Question: How many NFL greats are in heaven?

$400 Answer: Truman, Eisenhower, Kennedy, Nixon, Johnson, Reagen

Question: How many Black presidents are in heaven? How many White?

$ 500 Answer: Rick James, Barry White, Luther Vandross, Ray Charles

Question: How many of these famous African Americans are in heaven?

$ 600 Answer: John Calvin, Martin Luther, Martin Luther King, Pope John Paul

Question: How many of these famous religious leaders are in heaven?

$ 700 Answer: The Civil War, World War II, Korea, Vietnam, Iraq

Question: How many killed, soldiers and civilians are in heaven?

$800 Answer: The 3,000 Americans who died on September 11, 2001

Question: How many people killed by terrorist are in heaven?

$900 Answer: The Native Americans, African Slaves, Ku Klux Klan Lynchings

Question: How many of these American victims are in heaven?

$ 1000 Answer: THANK YOU JEHOVAH!!

Question: HOW MANY OF THE PEOPLE LISTED ABOVE WILL

NOT HAVE TWO CHANCES OF BEING RESURRECTED?

NONE OF THEM!! WHAT A LOVING GOD!!

CHAPTER TWENTY FOUR

"BONE OF MY BONES, FLESH OF MY FLESH"

The first time a man laid eyes on a female, he uttered the words above. Gender was introduced into the human family. " Male and female he created them." "Further God blessed them and said "Be fruitful and become many." Femininity, came into existence for the first time among intelligent creatures. The angels in heaven do not reproduce. Without females, there is no sex in heaven. The next time you hug your wife think of that. Yes the angels in heaven, had never seen a woman before. Genesis 2: 25 states: "and both of them continued to be naked, the man and his wife." Adam and Eve were married, and were commanded to have children. So the original sin in the Garden of Eden was not, Adam having sexual relations with Eve. How were they going to have children? One man and woman with an assignment from God. Make BABIES!!

How long would it take Adam, and his wife Eve to : "fill the earth and subdue it?" (Genesis 2: 28) Let's say 3 billion humans, half the current population of the earth. It would have taken Adam and Eve, and their future offspring, perhaps 2,000 years or more. Talk about a non-stop party! Everyone one of those children, would be born perfect. No vaccinations, no chicken pox, no mumps, no measles, not even a cold! What a prospect lay ahead, for the first human pair. The only two people on earth, with no belly buttons!! Here comes Adam, and the mother of the human race, Eve.

I love women! Good-looking, soft spoken, gentle, delicate, and precious. Under that beautiful exterior, is a "people factory"! I am not implying women have only a single purpose. That would be demeaning. You have to admit, that no one does it better. If a young girl reaches puberty at 13, and goes through menopause at age 50. Even if she never has children. Her body has prepared itself, over 400 times to make a baby. It's called a menstrual cycle. All it takes is a drop of male sperm, and the factory springs to life. From that point on, the whole process is automatic. There is no check-list, for new borns. If you don't have it, when you slide down the birth canal. You don't have it! What if babies came like kids furniture? (Some assembly required) There would be some strange looking kids in kindergarten. " What happened to you?" " My dad didn't read the instructions!" Ask a pregnant woman; "What part of the baby is developing today?" Would she reply? " Oh today I'm making toes and fingernails, and tomorrow I start with the elbows and knee caps!" (She has no idea) Women know as much about making babies, as I do about growing a beard. If I don't shave, here it comes.

Females have what I call, "baby software". Try this test: name five characteristics that women have which men do not have. But they have nothing to do with child-bearing, or nursing children. Here's one: Women have softer higher voices! Give me four more.

CHAPTER TWENTY FIVE

ORGANS FOR REPRODUCTION--NOT JUST SEX

A person is standing behind a sheer curtain. Is it a man or woman? Look for the baby software. Breast, (I wish they were retractable), hips that curve, rounded shoulders and butts. Then the hidden software, fallopian tubes, eggs, wombs, menstrual cycles etc. All for what? Just to drive men crazy? Is there some alternative function, or purpose for women's breast? (Breast: a milk delivery apparatus for babies, but grown men like them too. Also called "boobs". Perhaps because they don't do much, unless you have a baby.) I asked a pregnant woman if she planned to breast feed. Her reply: "Are you kidding?" Excuse me lady, I didn't mean to offend you. I always thought that was why God gave women breast. Oh I get it: "That baby should be glad, you didn't excercise your constitutional right to have an abortion." "Let him suck on his fingers, and be thankful!"

IS IT AN AUTOMOBILE OR A FLOWER POT?

If you purchased a convertible car, and parked it in a sunny location. Then you filled up the interior with dirt, and added miracle-grow. If you planted tulips, and sold them at a flower shop. Would that make the convertible, a flower pot? Perhaps, but what a waste. Why does a flower pot need a transmission, tires, a radio, air conditioning, bucket seats, headlights, etc. The designer, or creator says what it is. He made it! Of course, after you purchase it, you have the right to use it anyway you want. But it remains what the designer made it to be. That is what it is called. My point?

I was watching a "Gay Pride" parade on the news. I saw thousands of women proclaiming their sexual orientation. But being a man, I can still see the "people factory". They have the "baby software", but they use it in a different way. There was a woman, with four adult children. Then she discovered she was gay. The average heterosexual woman, has two children. But a lesbian, has four kids?

We do not have sex organs. They are reproductive organs. Six billion people alive on earth today. How many have already died? Perhaps 10 billion? All sixteen billion were conceived, and born one way. Your mother carried you in her womb, until you were born. At birth the doctor says: 'It's a boy or a girl!" Sex has something to do with reproduction, at least a small part. You will never see a baby born, in a pornographic movie. As if there was no connection between sex and children. Humans are not flower pots. You were made for a purpose, not an alternative. That's the truth.

CHAPTER TWENTY SIX

"LOVERS OF THEMSELVES, MONEY, AND PLEASURES"

These are just three of more than fifteen, negative qualities described at 2 Timothy 3:1-5. The selfish, pleasure seeking attitude of people in general. Would be proof we are living in "the Last Days". Before what? God destroys this wicked world.

(Fictional Case) A lady was jogging one day, and in the distance she could hear a baby crying. The sound became louder as she came near a trash container. Under the cover, and inside was a newborn baby. She started to sing a little song: "Ahhhhh, who would do that to a little baby?" This same woman who climbed into a dumpster, to save a strangers baby. Might choose to abort or abandon her own child, in the future. The woman whose baby was thankfully found in the dumpster, is at work at the World Trade Center on September 11, 2001. Her office on the 102nd floor, is jolted from the impact of a Boeing 767, ten stories below. She runs to the roof of the building, and frantically calls for help. Where is her guardian angel? If God notices a mere sparrow that falls to the ground. He had to see those two jumbo jets, right? Yes he saw them! God sometimes works in mysterious ways, right? Wrong, dead wrong! How many of the women and men who worked at the World Trade Center, were pro-choice? How many women who had gotten abortions, would not hesitate to get another one, or would gladly drive a workmate to get an abortion? All those women, including the lady who threw her baby in the dumpster. They find it mysterious, that God didn't send the angels to save them? That is obvious, not mysterious! God did not save the good people, who worked at the Twin Towers.

He should save those who are : "Lovers of themselves, lovers of money, lovers of pleasure, rather than lovers of God?" The simple truth.

CHAPTER TWENTY SEVEN

WHAT IS "HELL"--AND IS IT HOT?

You hear that a good friend of yours, "got fired." What comes to your mind, fire, heat, pain, or even torture? Not at all. It simply means terminated. For God who is immortal, and can never die. The worst punishment, is non-existence. Not pain and suffering. NBA, (National Baskeball Association) coaches, are never released, or laid-off. They all get fired! Did just his body get fired, but his soul is still the coach? Of course not. So when God fires someone, you simply die. Body and soul. 'Fear him which is able to destroy both soul and body in Hell" Matthew 10: 28 K. J.

T. D. JAKES IS GOING TO "HELL"--JESUS DID

So am I! So what's the big deal? The cover of a national news journal asked: "Is T. D. Jakes-The next Billy Graham? Many born again Christians, don't believe they are going to "HELL". As if that condition was beneath them.

The Bible speaks of Jonah, King David, and even Jesus as being in Hell. For example, Jonah fearing that inside of a huge fish was going to be his final resting place. "out of the belly of HELL, cried I" (Jonah 2: 3 K. J.) There was no fire, or torture. In fact Jonah was not even dead yet. He thought that his Hell, or grave was going to be inside of that fish. King David did not fear being tormented in Hell. Instead he said: "my heart is glad, and my glory rejoiceth. For thou wilt not leave my soul in HELL" (Psalms 16: 9, 10 K. J.) On the day of Pentecost, Peter quoted from Psalms 16 and applied it to the resurrected Jesus. Acts 2: 31 says: "he [spoke] of the resurrection of Christ, that his soul was not left in HELL. If Jesus went to Hell, then T. D. Jakes has no cause for offense in my saying truthfully. That he is going to HELL. Then God can decide if, like Jesus, he is deserving of going to heaven. Please note: Acts 2: 34 'For David did not ascend into the heavens." Wow king David went to HELL, and did not ascend into heaven. No worry, he still has two chances of being resurrected. Most likely as a "righteous" person. (Acts 24: 15) Is T. D. Jakes better than King David? Am I better than king David? NO!! And neither are you. Can you handle the TRUTH?

A BRIEF HISTORY OF THE WORD "HELL"

According to the New International Dictionary, unabridged. Under "Hell" it says: The word "hell" thus originally conveyed no thought of heat or torment, but simply of a 'covered over or concealed place'. In the old English dialect the expression, "helling potatoes" meant not to roast them, but simply to place the potatoes in the ground or in a cellar." That's the TRUTH!!

CHAPTER TWENTY EIGHT

Where Is The Fear Of God?

"**A** son for his part honors his father, and a servant his grand master. So if I am a father where is the honor of me? And if I am a grand master, WHERE IS THE FEAR OF ME? The Israelites save the healthy animals to use for their food, and to work their farms. Then offer the "blind", "lame", and "sick" animals to God! "In what way have we polluted you?" (Malachi 6: 8) Keep the sound animals for themselves, and offer the crappy ones to God. Where was their "fear of God?"

What four-letter word, is used more than 200 times in the Bible? Use that word to complete this sentence. "Come ye children...I will teach you the _ _ _ _ of the Lord" (Psalms 34: 11) No not love, F-E-A-R is the correct word. Psalms 111: 10 says "The fear of the Lord is the beginning of Wisdom." Job 28: 28 says: "the fear of the lord, that is wisdom" Then Proverbs 1: 7 states: "The fear of the Lord is the beginning of knowledge." K. J. Can we find the 'Fear of God" in our day?

WHERE IS THE FEAR OF GOD?

I was watching "Oprah", for maybe the fourth or fifth time since it has been on television. (I like Oprah Winfrey, but I'm still at work at 3PM Monday to Friday) This beautiful black actress was Oprah's guest today. She had just been through her second, painful, messy, and very public divorce. She declared on national television: "I am never getting married again" Was the "finest woman on the planet", (Arsenio Hall quote) giving up sex? She did not elaborate. I think she meant just matrimony. She does want children, but she will never marry again. Then she says: "Well Oprah, you never married!" (Oh yes Stedman) I thought to myself. None of my business what people do in their personal lives. This was on television, so I wondered.

What if this actress proclaimed on national television: "I will never renew my California driver license again." What would happen, the day after her driver's license expired. The police, and several T. V camera crews, would be parked outside her front door. Waiting to see if she has the audacity, to get in her car and drive away. After such a public statement, would she risk repeated fines, and eventual imprisonment for breaking California laws? Never happen! She would be afraid! Yet this beautiful woman in her mid 30's, (unless she took a vow of celibacy) has no qualms about practicing fornication. For the rest of her adult life? No worry of repercussions?

Andrew Young, a close friend of Dr. Martin Luther King. When asked by a television anchor-woman, about alledged extra-marital affairs, of Dr. King. Neither denied, nor defended his infidelity. "Martin had a fondness for women!" he calmly replied. Are we fooling ourselves? Or is everything 0. K.? I have my doubts!

More than once the Bible says that "fornicators will not inherit God's kingdom" Yet no on seems to have the "fear of God". One black basketball player, once claimed in his autobiography, to have slept with more than 10,000 women. (Or 20,000) A born again Christian, himself a former Harlem Globetrotter. Delivered a glowing eulogy for his former colleague. I ask, where is the "fear of God"? In the book of Numbers, God killed 24,000 Israelites in one day. They had committed fornication, one time. (Numbers 25: 9) I sit in judgement of no one! But has God changed his mind about fornication?

Ecclesiastes 8:12 warns: "Although a sinner may be doing bad a hundred times, and continuing a long time as he pleases, yet I am aware that it will turn out well with those FEARING the [true] God, because they are in fear of him. But it will not turn out well at all for the wicked, neither will he prolong his days that are like a shadow, because he is not in FEAR of God." Why does no one change his ways, if those words are true?

We fear and respect the laws of humans, but not the laws of God. Why? Ecclesiastes 8: 11 gives a possible reason: "Because sentence against a bad work has not been executed speedily, that is why the hearts of the sons of men, has become fully set in them, to do bad." So I ask again: " Where is the FEAR of the grand master?"

Most people whether they are religious are not claim to believe in God. James 2: 19 states: "You believe in God, do you? You are doing quite well. Yet the demons believe and shudder." As in fear? The future king of God's kingdom was prophesied about at Isaiah 11: 2, 3: "and upon him the spirit of Jehovah must settle down, the spirit of wisdom and of understanding, the spirit of counsel and mightiness, the spirit of knowledge and of the fear of Jehovah; and there will be ENJOYMENT by him in the fear of Jehovah." Jesus himself finds enjoyment in "the fear of the Lord". We should too!

CHAPTER TWENTY NINE

YOU MUST LOVE GOD-FIRST!!

Which is more important then, to love God or to fear him? It is not which one is needed the most. Both are equally essential. It is the order of progression that is the key. Jesus said at Mark 12: 29 'The FIRST of all commandments is...verse 30: And thou shalt Love the Lord thy God with all thy heart,...soul...mind....and with all thy strength." Think about this however; You cannot love someone you do not know. But you can worship someone you do not know. To the Samaritan woman Jesus said: "You worship what you do not know, we worship what we know." (John 4: 22) Pop stars like Britney Spears or Justin Timberlake are worshipped, or idolized by millions of adoring fans. But they have never met, Britney or Justin, and most of them never will. The idols of today are not made of gold, wood, or stone. Todays idols are human, flesh and blood, tattoos, throw-back jerseys, timberland boots, and spiked hairdo's. People worship super-stars they don't know, and who don't know or care about them. Other than buying their records, and baskeball shoes. In order to love someone you must know them, and they have to know you also. Galations 4: 9 N W. states: But now that you have come to know God, or rather now that you have come to be known by God." Humans like Saul, before he became the apostle Paul. Can be grossly mistaken in their beliefs, and yet have: "a zeal for God, but not according to [accurate] knowledge." (Romans 10: 2) The result? They would persecute, and even murder in the name of God. Jesus warned his apostles: "the time cometh, that whosoever killeth you will think he doeth God's service..These things will they do unto you, because they have not KNOWN the father, nor me" (John 16: 2, 3)

ACCURATE KNOWLEDGE= LOVE

THE APPLICATION OF KNOWLEDGE= WISDOM

THE BEGINNING OF WISDOM= "THE FEAR OF THE LORD"

CHAPTER THIRTY

"I LOVE YOU, BUT I DON'T LIKE YOU"

With only one English word for love. It can be difficult to express the different facets or types of love. People will add a pre-fix such as "tough love", or "puppy love". In the Greek language there are four distinct words for l-o-v-e. E'ros, for love between the sexes is not used in the Greek scriptures. (New Testament) Phi'lia, as in brotherly love, from which the city of Philadelphia get's it's name. Stor-ge' is the third Greek word for love. Also there is a-ga'pe, which appears more frequently than the other terms. Because of the limtations of English, many Christians really don't fully understand what a-ga'pe love means. I used to have this favorite saying: "Jesus commanded that you love your brothers, he didn't say you had to like them." "What a terrible thing for a person to say. You see, I like everybody! And you know what else? Everybody Likes Me.!!" (Huh! That's What He Thinks!)

Think about this: "Why would Jesus need to COMMAND, that you love someone. If you already liked them, in the first place?" You don't need to be commanded, to love your mother! To Illustrate: You loan two people $500 dollars. The one who repays the loan on time, and in full. Do you need to be commanded to love him? No it's easy to love him. Because you have your money, back in your pocket! Now the other person. You also loaned him $500 dollars. But two years later, he has not repaid a single dime. Then you see him at church. He has on a brand new suit!! Now, which of those two people, do you need to be COMMANDED, to love? Obviously, the one in the new suit. Now answer this: Do you like him? Truthfully, do you like him? Of course you don't! But you can still love him! How? By not kidnapping his kids, or slashing his tires. Psalms 37: 21 states: "The wicked one is borrowing, and does not pay back." Are we as Christians commanded to like, wicked people? No indeed. A-ga'pe means: You show a individual love, even if you don't particulary like what he did to you.

Professor William Barclay, in his New Testament words says: Agap'e has to do with the mind. It is not an emotion which rises unbidden from our hearts, [as may be the case with phi-li'a] it is a principle by which we deliberately live. Agap'e, has supremely to do with the will. It is a conquest, a victory, and achievement. No one ever naturally loved his enemies. To love one's enemies is a conquest of all our natural inclinations and emotions. This agap'e...is in fact the power to love the unloveable, to love people whom WE DO NOT LIKE. AMEN!! When John 3:16 says "God Loved the World so much he gave his son" Many think: "Boy, God must really like us humans!" Nothing could be further from the truth. Psalms 97: 10 urges: "Ye that love the lord, hate evil" We are commanded to hate evil, because God does. He also has the power to love the unloveable. Which he has done since the creation of mankind.

CHAPTER THIRTY ONE

GOD BLESS AMERICA!!--PLEASE?

"God Bless America!! And nobody else!! (From a recent movie) There is one problem with this common expression. It never includes the word, "please". "God, Please Bless America." That is a humble request. Without the the please, it is a command! In several areas, the technology of the United States is without equal. Militarily, and monetarily, America has no real rivals. What about morally? Not in human eyes, but in the eyes of God. A typical daily newspaper reports on all kinds of events, good and bad. Thousands of people every year get rich in America. But sadly, thousands of people are victimized also. Are you more likely to get rich, or get cheated? Nothing really bad has ever happened to me in America. That wasn't at least partly my fault. Others have not been so fortunate. In fact during the eight year term of a recent President. Over 90,000 Americans were murdered. One million American women reported being raped. Twice that number were raped, but did not report it. When a candidate is nominated for the Supreme court. The first question seems to be, will he repeal Roe vs. Wade. What about his ability, honesty, or integrity? Can we find out if he's a nice guy first? "No, he might not let me murder my kids" Two of the most vocal groups today. Pro-choice and gay rights proponents, receive a lot of media coverage. So I ask: "Is America truly the greatest nation on earth, under God?" Which God? 2 Corinthians 4: 4 speaks of: "the God of this world." Referring to the Devil.

May the "only true God" (John 17: 3) Bless America, and Everybody else!!

JUDGEMENT DAY

What would be the purpose of resurrecting a individual, who had been dead for a thousand years. Only to have him stand before the "throne of God" and hear all of sins rehashed in detail. "Lord, you could have left me in the grave!" Talk about holding a grudge? What about a statute of "Limitations"? There is according to Romans 6: 7 "He that has died is freed from sin" Say that again? "For he who has died has been acquitted from [his] sin. N. W. So when Jesus said: "All those in the memorial tombs will hear his voice and come out." (That is the resurrection of the "righteous and unrighteous") Then if you do good things after your resurrection, how will it turn out to be? John 5: 28, 29 "a resurrection of LIFE" But what if you do bad things, even after being acquited and resurrected? The result is: "A resurrection of JUDGEMENT" How about that for a God of Love. To be resurrected, with a clean slate so to speak. Then a genuine opportunity to gain everlasting life. For most it will be their first chance, to come to know the "true God". "Because he hath appointed a day, in the which he will judge the world in righteousness." Acts 17: 30 "Judgement Day", will be a happy day for all mankind!

CHAPTER THIRTY TWO

WILL YOU FIND THE TRUTH THAT SETS YOU FREE?

For many, these so-called truths are just opinions or ramblings of an ex-drunk. "He got sober, then he got religious!" Could I be wrong? Of course any imperfect human can be sincerely mistaken. However, if the truth is impossible to find. How could a just God, destroy people for not finding "the Truth?" Jesus said it would be difficult. Referring to the "wheat" of truth, and the "weeds" of lies. Matthew 13: 30 says: "Let them grow together until the harvest." Verse 39 continues: "The harvest is a conclusion of a system of things, and the reapers are angels." The angels would separate the "wheat from the weeds". Yes we have invisible help. But we also have an invisible enemy, the Devil. That is why you must study the Bible daily. The fact that God has not already destroyed this world. Can only mean one thing. Salvation is still possible.

"Let yor utterances be always with graciousness, seasoned with salt." (Colossians 4: 6) I had to be brutally honest in order, to get sober. So sometimes I can be a little too blunt in trying to make a point. Please add a little salt to my words. But do not water them down. Even if you disagree with some statements, that's fine. Thank you for listening to my story of a "spiritual awakening". I continue to "search for God"!

Your search for the truth, may be similar to the apostle Paul's experiences. Acts 17: 2, 3 says: "he went to them, and for three sabbaths he reasoned with them from the scriptures, explaining and proving by references that is was necessary for the Christ to suffer." Acts 17: 4 continues: "As a result some of them became believers and associated themselves with Paul and Silas." Then Acts 17: 5 states: "But the Jews became jealous...formed a mob and proceeded to throw the city into an uproar." "They indeed agitated the crowd and the city rulers, when they heard these things." (Acts 17: 8) "The brothers sent both Paul and Silas to Beroea..." "Now the latter were more noble-minded than those in Thessalonica, for they received the word with the greatest eagerness of mind, carefully examining the scriptures daily, as to whether these things were so." (Acts 17: 10,11) Satan the Devil, knows the truth! May you find the "the truth that sets you free", and also makes you happy! "For whoso findeth me, findeth LIFE!" Proverbs 8: 35

Thomas John Ford

E-Mail: Bigjohn2520@hotmail.com

CHAPTER THIRTY THREE

HAVE YOU EVER WONDERED ABOUT THIS?

THE CROSS: If someone you loved was murdered. If they were stabbed, shot, strangled, or killed by a drunk driver. Would you wear a small knife around your neck? What about a small gold-plated pistol? Who would hang a can of "Bud", on a chain around their neck? Is that how you would want to remember, your son or daughter? What family would request to have copies, of the police crime scene photos. After a close relative was brutally murdered? The pictures would be too painful, to look at.! When the mailman came with a package, what would he think? "You have a picture of your murdered daughter, lying in a pool of blood? On your living room wall?"

CRUCIFIX; definition; a cross with the figure of Jesus crucified upon it.

When I stopped at a red light. On the rear of this car was a figure of a child, who was kneeling before "Jesus Cross". "Oh, how touching!" In a recent movie, a ruthless, foul-mouthed, rogue cop. Wore a cross, along with his police shield as he yelled: "I'm the mother_ _** police." This drug dealer in a police surveilance video, also had a cross around his neck. How many hip-hop artist wear a cross, as they shout the most obscene lyrics ever recorded? There are a thousand shapes in which to design jewelry. Why is the cross number one? The people who make and sell the Cross, love Jesus? The people who wear them, and put them on car bumpers. They love and respect Jesus Christ?

I Wonder: WHO BELIEVED IN THE TRINITY FIRST?

Egyptian Triad: Horus, Osiris, and Isis 2nd millennium B.C.E.

Babylonian Triad: Ishtar, Sin, Shamash 2nd millennium B.C.E.

Ancient Palmyra Triad: Moon God, Sun God, Lord of the Heavens 1st cent.C.E.

"Many centuries before the time of Christ, there were triads, or trinities of gods in ancient Babylonia, and Assyria" (The French: "Larousse Encyclopedia of Mythology")

"ONE SEATED ON THE THRONE"--NOT THREE

Revelation 4: 2 "and ONE sat on the throne K. J.

Revelation 4:9: "Thanksgiving to the ONE seated upon the throne N.W.

Revelation 4:10 "twenty-four elders fall..before..ONE seated on throne" N.W.

Revelation 5: 1 A scroll "in the right hand of the ONE seated on the throne" N.W.

Revelation 5: 7 The Lamb took the scroll: "out of the right hand of the ONE seated on the throne." I wonder about the Trinity, do you?

CHAPTER THIRTY FOUR

ESSAY
"YOU WILL REAP WHAT YOU SOW"

How will you ever be content, under the humble kingdom of God? After living in a modern society. Where everything is either, automatic, self-winding, pre-sweetened, permanent-pressed, steel-belted, or is in Dvd, or on CD, for my Suv! Where people live in open defiance of God's clear warning; "whatsoever a man soeth, that shall he also reap." No one seems to worry about that warning, from God. So how do we know for sure, that "you reap what you sow?" Read Galations 6: 7. Question? What did God say before the warning, you will reap what you sow? The answer: "Do not be misled, God is not one to be mocked. For whatever a man is sowing, this will he also reap." N.W. How do we know, that you will reap what you sow? BECAUSE YOU CAN'T MOCK GOD!

We will ask a series of questions. Some of them we will answer for you. Some, you must answer for yourself. We will also offer some counsel and advice. Today, most people don't welcome or appreciate, you giving them counsel or advice. I read once where this professor said: "I don't give advice anymore! Because the wise men don't need it. And the fools won't HEED it". Whether you are wise or foolish, is up to you! Our first question: Will you be happy to reap, what you are now sowing? God created humans, but he didn't create "human nature". Ever notice that humans rarely defy God's physical laws? Who would jump from a airplane, without a parachute, but hoping: "Maybe this time I'll just bounce along." Who picks wild mushrooms, and puts them on his childs slice of pizza? They might be poisonous, but

79

they might not be! But who would take the chance? No One!! There is a reason why humans respect God's physical laws. They are enforced instantly, automatically, and indiscriminately. You can jump off a cliff. Or slip and fall from a cliff. One is called a suicide. One is called an accident. But they both mean-DEAD! People steer clear of defying, God's physical laws. However, when it comes to God's moral laws: fornication, adultery, homosexuality, lying, stealing and so on. Because there is no immediate punishment as in the case of gravity. People fool themselves into thinking. Maybe I won't reap what I sow. Is that the case? No! Why not? Because you: "Can't Mock God!"

Second question: Will more people be surprised they made it to heaven? Or will more people be surprised they didn't make it to heaven? A surprise is something unexpected, or usually undeserved. The correct answer is: No one will be SURPRISED, he made it to heaven. When a farmer cultivates the soil, and then plants corn seeds. In the harvest season, when he looks out of his window. If he saw corn growing, would he be surprised? If he saw tomatoes growing he would be surprised, and angry too! You expect to reap, exactly what you have sown. Farming however, comes with no guarantees. You could plant the best seed, in the best soil. Then due to circumstances beyond your control: Wind, rain, drought, insect, illness, accidents, etc. For all the hard work and effort he sowed. He could reap, absolutely nothing!

Notice the promise that God gives: Galations 6: 9 "for in due season we shall reap, if we faint not." K.J. If you are faithful, you shall "reap what you sow!" God will not mock himself, by failing to do what he promised.

Third question: What does it mean to "Find" the road to life? (Matthew 7: 14) To find something, does not simply mean to locate, or pick it up. You must appreciate, or recognize the VALUE, of what you find. Jesus gave two examples at Matthew 13: 44, 46. A man finds a treasure in a field, also he finds a pearl. In both cases he knows or appreciates, the VALUE of what he has found. It is worth more than anything he already owns. If a man living today, found an old Eisenhower silver dollar. He pays for his morning newspaper, with the coin he just found. The cashier happens to be a coin collector. She looks at the date on the coin, and her face lights up! She begins to jump around in circles. Too much caffeine? The coin you just gave away, is worth $500 hundred dollars. You picked up the coin, but you didn't FIND it! You did not appreciate, or recognize the true VALUE of the coin. The majority of mankind are on the "road to destruction". Just a few said Jesus would find the "narrow way" to life. Most of the people on the road to destruction, have more than once "picked up" a pearl of high VALUE. But they failed to recognize it. "I already found the road to "Life". So they throw away the treasure of everlasting life. It was right in their hands!

Fourth question: Do you fully believe, that you will reap, what you are now sowing? Why such a question? Because humans tend to excuse, or even deceive themselves. Galations 6: 3 says: "For if a man think himself something, when he is nothing, he deceiveth himself." K. J. Or, "he is deceiving his own mind" N.W. A Christian may rationalize: "I think I'm a pretty nice person. I'm certainly not a wicked person. I should make it into heaven." I will admit, there are some rewards that may come your way for just being a nice person. But everlasting life, is not one of them!

Ever notice when vacation time comes. You never seem to have enough money saved. Those are the two "brokest" weeks of the year for many. So for next year's vacation, you go out and buy a piggy bank. Then you and your wife promise to save $20 dollars a week. That means a thousand bucks to spend for vacation. You start out great, saving every week. Then guess what: "Luther Vandross got a new CD!" "Honey, let's skip this week, and double up next week!" That only happens a few times, during the year. Or so you think. Well vacation time finally comes. You pack your luggage, and load up the car. You look over your maps. Now it's time to crack open the piggy bank! So you open the piggy bank, and count the money. "Hey honey, call the police, we been robbed!! "I know we saved more money than this!" Remember our two questions? Will you be happy to reap what you are now sowing? And. Do you fully believe, that you will reap what you are now sowing? You need to answer honestly. Why? BECAUSE YOU CAN'T MOCK GOD! The Christian way of life, is like a piggy bank. What you put into it, is what you get out of it. Here's hoping you'll be happy, yes that you'll be proud to "reap what you have sown".

Isaiah 48: 17 says: "I am the lord thy God, which teacheth thee to profit" K.J. We profit, or benefit in what ways? Spiritually, physically, and even financially. Let's look at three areas. Drinking, smoking, and immorality! Have you been to a liquor store lately? Do you know how much a good bottle of liquor cost? The expression: "Wino's don't start out drinking Ripple!" is true. Getting drunk everyday, put a ripple in their wallet. Proverbs 23: 21 warns: For the drunkard and the glutton shall come to poverty." Drinking in moderation, or not at all, means a "profit" for you.

How about smoking? In California, if you smoke two packs of cigarettes a day. By the end of the year, you have spent more than $2,000 dollars. Up in smoke! If your neighbor who smokes. Saw you put $2,000 dollars in a garbage can, and set it on fire. What would he say? (Besides you're crazy) "Why instead of burning up good money like that, you could give that money to me." Well neighbor, you could stop smoking, and give that money to me. You profit yourself by not smoking.

What about immorality? Without going into a lot of lurid details. Here's a simple fact. If you have a wife. And you have a girlfriend. Women cost money!! And two women cost twice the money. You profit yourself, spiritually, physically, and even financially. It cost money to be a wicked person. One day it may cost your life. How can you be sure? BECAUSE YOU CAN'T MOCK GOD!!

Final question: Who are the fornicators, that will not inherit God's kingdom? Jesus gave a clue in the sermon on the mount. Matthew 5: 28 says: "Whosoever looketh on a woman to lust after her, hath committed adultery with her already in his heart." (Only a married man could commit adultery in his heart) He may claim faithfulness to his spouse, as long as he never actually touches her body sexually. His wife would have no grounds for divorce, until he committed the actual act. Jesus however, can read hearts, thoughts, and intentions. Would Jesus have to wait until you stole his wallet, to know you are a thief? Not at all! The news program "Dateline" ran a survey that asked: "If you could steal $10.000 and no one would find out. Would you do it? The number one reply? "Show me the money!" No harm, it's just a survey. Yes, but your answer reveals what is in your heart. Even if you have never stolen a single thing in your life. If you would steal something, as long as nobody found out about it. You are a thief! Example: Which is a man first? Is he a pick-pocket first, or is he a thief first? The man is a thief first. If he wasn't already a thief. His hand would not be in your pocket, in the first place. Thieves also, will not inherit God's kingdom. It has to do with what you are, in your heart. Who then are the fornicators, that will not inherit God's kingdom? Those who are fornicators in their hearts. Even if they NEVER actually commit the act. Proverbs 4: 23 says: "More than all else that is to be guarded, safeguard your heart."

So in conclusion I ask: " What will you do the next time you hear someone, quote or paraphrase Galations 6: 7: " For whatever a man is sowing, this he will also reap.?" I hope you ask them if they know why? If they don't know, please tell them.

"BECAUSE YOU CAN'T MOCK GOD" If you however, think deeply and apply the Bible principles discussed. You can look forward to a future, where you won't be surprised! But here's hoping you'll be happy. Yes that you'll be proud!!

TO "REAP WHAT YOU HAVE SOWN!!"

CHAPTER THIRTY FIVE

ESSAY
"DOES YOUR THINKING AGREE WITH GOD'S?"

As you sit, perhaps in the comfort of your living room. There are at the same moment, nearly two million Americans sitting in prison. This is the so-called "land of the free?" What one word would you use to describe the difference, between yourself and someone in prison. "Conduct!" They did something, or they wouldn't be in jail! "Association!" Hanging out with the wrong crowd, can lead to disaster. "Education!" Or the lack of it does appear to lead to crime. "Poverty!" That also is related to criminal activity. The correct answer though is: "THINKING" "The difference between right action, and wrong action is thought. What you think, determines what you do." Those are the words of Jack D. Redford, a Bible scholar now deceased. He was also a seminary school instructor. At the graduation he concluded his speech to the class by stating: "There are many very intelligent people in the world, who are poor thinkers. There are many people of average intelligence who have become skilled thinkers. So acquire that skill!" God is the greatest thinker in the universe. We humans can learn much.

Sadly, most people don't like being told what to do. Even worse what to think. "That is mind control!" They protest! Can we agree on this simple premise? You rarely do something well, the very first time you try it. Can you remember the first time you went to a bowling alley. Did you bowl a 300 game? Of course not, you were terrible. In order to improve at something, often people will take lessons. Swimming

84

lessons, golf, tennis, singing, ballet etc. Do we need lessons on how to live? None of us have lived before. This is a first time experience. So how do you expect to do well, without some instructions? But all too often you hear: "It's his life, let him live it anyway he wants!" If you take swimming lessons, before you jump into a 20 foot deep pool. Why do we need no instructions on living, before jumping into the "ocean of life"?

Just because you have life. Does not mean, that you know how to live. You can possess something, and still not know how to use it. Did you ever own a VCR, but could not record a T. V. show? You owned a computer, but could not program it. How many people have a driver's license? (But can't drive a lick) When it comes to driving an automobile, teenagers are a paradox. They have the best eye sight, reflexes, and co-ordination. They are also the most dangerous driver's on the road. Worse than even elderly driver's. (Insurance Company Data) They THINK, they know how to drive! However the number one cause of death for teenagers? Automobile Accidents!!

Not surprising, because of the lack of driving experience by teenagers. What did come as a shock, is the number three cause of death among teenagers. Suicide!! They also think they know how to "steer" their way in life, with little experience. "I do my own thing! You lived your life dad, don't tell me how to live mine!" I have a niece who says to me while driving: "Uncle tommy, I got this! I got this" (Talk to the hand, talk to the hand) Here is a simple list. If no one taught you these things, raise your hand.

Did someone teach you how to walk, or how to talk, to read, to write, to tie your shoes, to ride a bicycle, to tie a neck-tie? Did your mother potty train you? What if she never did? Then you showed up for the first grade wearing a diaper. You would have a nickname for life. "Here come's the "diaper boy." If you had to be taught those simple tasks. Why do you need no instruction, on how to live your life? You have never lived before! If your father was a pilot, and he gave you a small propeller plane. Would you gladly accept the free flight lessons, that came with the plane? Or would your attitude be: 'Thanks dad, but I don't need you to tell me how to fly my airplane!" That is what most humans do. They gladly accept the "gift of life" from God. Then reject the free instructions he gives, for a happy and safe journey through life. Sadly everyday we see people "crash and burn". Because their thinking did not agree with God's.

What word would describe a person, who jumped into an airplane. They had never flown an airplane before. Without any prior flight instruction, they just "take off"! Does the word rhyme with "Cupid"? Notice what word the creator uses, for those who jump into the "cockpit" of life. And attempt to fly on their own. Now at 15,000 feet they realize: "I don't know how to land!" They cry out to God, but will he answer? Proverbs 1: 22 says: "How long will you STUPID ones keep hating knowledge?" Verse 28 continues: "At that time they will keep calling me, but I shall not answer, they will keep looking for me, but they will not find me." Proverbs 1:32 concludes "the prosperity of fools will destroy them," K. J. Does the fact that you don't know how to fly an airplane, make you a fool or stupid. Not at all! However to think you can navigate your way through life smoothly. After rejecting the help of God! That is stupid. "He that is trusting in his own heart is STUPID" Proverbs 28: 25

THEIR THINKING DID NOT AGREE WITH GOD'S

Jesus said: "You have made the word of God invalid, because of your tradition." (Matthew 15: 6) The pharisees thought they were improving, and expounding the law. True story: In Elizabeth, New Jersey there was a bad intersection. Right by the Alexian Brothers Hospital. Even after four-way stop signs were installed, the accidents continued. Then someone came up with the bright idea: "Install signs that say FULL-STOP!" Did it solve the problem? NO! By installing signs that said: FULL-STOP, it made all the regular stop signs invalid. By adding a single word? Yes! What is a FULL-stop? Stop means stop! If someone was hitting you with a bat, and you said: STOP! Do you want them to slow down. Look both ways, and continue?

So we may have good intentions. However the results could be disastrous, like the Pharisees. If your thinking does not agree with God's

COMPUTER THINKING: Artificial intelligence. Does it work in actual practice? The following question was presented to a computer. You have two identical watches, one has completely stopped. The other works but it loses six minutes a day. Which watch is better? The stopped watch was better, according to the computer. Though not working, it at least had the correct time twice every 24 hours. The running watch never had the correct time, so it was useless. Are you looking forward to world run exclusively by computers? With that kind of logic? Not me.

The apostle Peter had deep love and affection for Jesus. On one occasion in particular it caused a problem. After telling his disciples: "He must go to Jerusalem and suffer many things...and be killed, and on the third day be raised up." (Matthew 16: 22, 23) Peter rebukes Jesus saying: "be kind to yourself lord, you will not have this [destiny] at all" But Jesus replies: "Get behind me Satan, because you think, not God's thoughts, but those of men." In Mark's account he notes that before Jesus rebuked Peter: "when he had turned about, and look on his disciples." (Mark 8: 33) Jesus words were not just meant for Peter, but all the apostles. Peter's heart was in the right place. However his thinking was not in agreement with God's.

"Seek first the kingdom and his righteousness." (Matthew 6: 33) The root word for righteousness is: "right". What is the advantage of doing something right? The advantage of doing something right, is that you only have to do it once.

The prophet Jonah's experience teaches us all a lesson. Jonah received an assignment: "Arise go to Ninevah, that great city, and cry against it." (Jonah 1:2) No way Jose' says Jonah. He hops a ship going in the opposite direction. Eventually he is swallowed by a giant fish. He spends three days inside of the fish. (It had to be very dark. What did it smell like inside the fish?) "The Lord [spoke] unto the fish, and it vomited out Jonah upon the dry ground." (Jonah 2: 10) What is the result, when you don't do something right the first time? You get to do it all over again. Jonah 3: 1 says: "The word of the Lord came unto Jonah the SECOND time. Arise, go unto Ninevah." The same assignment he originally received! The advantage of doing something right, is that you only have to do it once. If your thinking agrees with God's. You will always do what is right, And you'll only have to do it ONCE!!

"There is a way that seemeth right unto a man, but the end thereof are the ways of death." Proverbs 16: 25

Thomas John Ford

E-Mail: Bigjohn2520@hotmail.com

ABOUT THE AUTHOR

A life long student of the Bible, and ordained minister. During the Vietnam War he earned a military exemption, from the Selective Service Administration. (Draft Board) The IV-D, "Minister of Divinity" classification. For a single, draft age male with no dependents. It was nearly impossible to obtain, before the age of 20.

Thomas, is a accomplished public lecturer, and writer. Former actor, and radio personality. He retired from the Orange County Transportation Authority in 2005. His candor, and sense of humor. Spring from his humble belief, that humankind is perhaps the "most embarassing" creation of God. Still in existence. "God Loves Us!" Yes, but does he like us? The angels in heaven have also observed the sinful activity of humans. Each morning in heaven, the burning question is always asked. What Time Do The Saints Come Marching In? "Hey!, Who said: "Who Cares"?

CPSIA information can be obtained at www.ICGtesting.com
Printed in the USA
LVOW12s1900110913

351675LV00004BA/206/P

9 781425 907952